Sikiru Usman

The Great Success Highway

novum pocket

© 2024 novum publishing

ISBN 978-3-99010-693-8
Cover photo:
Bualong Sadsana | Dreamstime.com
Cover design, layout & typesetting:
novum publishing

www.novum-publishing.co.uk

Contents

IN HONOUR AND GLORY

Of

THE GREAT CREATOR,

THE ABSOLUTE, ALMIGHTY KING

Of

ALL REALMS OF LIFE

IN ETERNITY!

GREETINGS!

Hi!... The **All-WISE**,... **Almighty CREATOR**,... **Our GOD**. *Most Definitely Alone* is the **Supreme Eternal KING!** The **Absolute Sublime RULER** of all Realms of Existence in all Eternity! In His Holy and Most Exalted **NAME**, I welcome you, fellow ***Success-seeker,*** to this **Joyful Exploratory Platform!** And I really believe that it is not at all by any casual, arbitrary chance whatever that *you* are reading or even listening to this book, precisely at this very moment because it is just the very *right time* for *that* to happen. And *why* do I say this? You may rightfully ask. Well, the real answer lies quite simply in the title of the book itself:

'THE *GREAT* SUCCESS HIGHWAY! –

PRINCIPLED WAY OF THE MOST-HIGH

PUREST SUREST PATH OF TRUE LASTING SUCCESS'

This will naturally attract *only* those people, the *kindred spirits,* who are very seriously searching for *Lasting Values, the natural fruits* of **TRUE LASTING SUCCESS**, in their own lives. And who are therefore eagerly seeking the ***Purest Surest Path*** upon which they will most certainly find those *Eternal Values*. Now, the *latter* very clearly suggests the fact that those *benefits* acquired by the *Success-seeker*, while diligently striving along this **Surest Path**, are quite *Supreme* and *Transcendental*, naturally *extending far beyond* one's lifetime on this Earth. And where exactly can one find the most *accurate guidance* towards his own **Purest Surest Path** of *Lasting Prosperity* in this life, if not in *that* which is *truly living, eternal,* and thereby also bearing *lasting benefits?*

THIS, dear *Success-seeker,* is precisely *all-exclusively* in the **Living WORD** of the **ALMIGHTY LORD. The Everlasting TRUTH.** Therefore, I reckon that you, as a serious *Success-seeker* most probably wish to use this book as an *aid* for finding *Permanent Prosperity* in your own life. And if *that* is really the case, then you do need to accept, *right now,* the Total *Personal Responsibility* for your entire journey on **The *GREAT* SUCCESS HIGHWAY**, the Principled **WAY** of the **MOST-HIGH,** which is the **Purest Surest Path** of *True Lasting* **SUCCESS**. For this *great quest* calls for one's very serious and sincere, constant and really strong volition, plus *total* submission of oneself to the high *Guidance, the great Leadership* of the *All-wise* **CREATOR.**

THIS strictly demands that one *must* firmly resolve to become a very *humble, diligent* **lifelong apprentice** of His Living **WORD**, through Which He most graciously grants the required help to all genuine *seekers* of **True Lasting SUCCESS,** who always strive fervently to *ask, seek* and *knock* for His divine Help in childlike humility. NOW, It is quite likely also that you might have already recognised this very *crucial necessity,* through your own personal *experiences,* in the course of your serious seeking. Very plainly speaking, the very *first step* that we have to take in order to pave the *sure way* for that divine Help of our **MAKER,** is for each one of us to strive very seriously and diligently to establish a *pure* and *true personal connection* with Him.

AND this is greatly facilitated by one's *direct, ardent* supplication to Him in a *childlike* and very *humble* manner for this to really happen. In addition to which, this must be one's *constant and consistent* efforts to absorb *aright, very clearly, correctly and completely,* the *true essence* of His *Living* **WORD** and make it all an *integral part* of one's inner being in order to thereby become a very solid *Stronghold* of His **WORD** and a *Pure Temple* of true reverential Worship. Let us not ever forget that the **Living WORD** of the **Almighty LORD** is intended to graciously *help all serious seekers of* **Light** *and* **Truth** to:

1. Correctly absorb the *true Knowledge* of **Life** and this great **Creation**, plus the **CUE Laws** of the **Holy Will** of the **Almighty CREATOR** operating therein. Plus the true *unique meaning* and *exact purpose* of our conscious existence therein.
2. Thereby develop ourselves *aright* and acquire full *self-consciousness,* a *living intuition* and *balanced conscience, maturity* with absolutely *free will, power and nobility.* All of which will enable us to be, live and work *diligently* always in exact accordance with the **CUE Laws** of the All-Wise, **Holy Will** of our **Great MAKER.**
3. Therein really absorb the *true knowledge* of the **Holy Will** of our Great **LORD** Himself. Which then, and

only then, affords us the great possibility of acquiring the exact knowledge of our **Almighty MAKER**, as far as it is humanly possible for us to know or perceive **Him.** This is what, in turn, then really makes the *right* form of *personal connection* with **Him** possible. And via which the *greatest joy ever,* of one's conscious life in this Creation, can arise!

4. Consequently, ascend progressively upwards to the pure luminous Kingdom, our origin, *Paradise,* where we can keep on living in *eternal joyful* and *harmonious co-operation*, in the *pure service* of the **Holy Will** of the **ALMIGHTY,** our **GOD!** Which is indeed the *ultimate eternal value* and *crown* of True Lasting **SUCCESS** in this life!

NOW, it is very true indeed that the Almighty **LORD** has been sending down to us, on this Earth, His *loving help* over the past thousands of years, quite vividly through the great manifestations of His *wonderful* **Creation** and, in the form of His **Living WORD** through His carefully chosen *Servant-Helpers*. That is, the *True Leaders* and *Teachers* of men, in a very gradual, orderly, systematic progression. These great ones included such *eminent personalities* like Hjalfdar, Krishna and Zoroaster, Laotse and Buddha, and the great Arabian Prophet Mohamed. Of very high significance also is the mission of the magnificent Bringer of the **Ten Commandments** of the **ALMIGHTY**, Moses.

And absolutely worthy of *reverential acknowledgement* indeed was the mission of pure Love, for the Salvation, Redemption and Joyful Ascent of all mankind, which was most graciously undertaken by the sublime *Truth Bringer,* **JESUS**… the **CHRIST**, down to this planet Earth, about two thousand years ago. **THE GOSPEL** of the **CHRIST**, **JESUS**, is widely available in *printed word form* on this Earth today, as a *very special* part of the several kinds of the **Holy Bible**, under the title of the ***New Testament***. What is *more recent* and also *newer* to us earthly humanity is the great Spiritual Work which is titled **'IN THE LIGHT OF TRUTH – THE GRAIL MESSAGE'** by **ABD-RU-SHIN,** Who in the *pure execution* of the perfect Divine Will of the **Almighty CREATOR**, Supreme **KING** of all Realms, has brought this *very wonderful* and *most enlightening* Message down for us.

The latter very clearly gives us a comprehensive perspective of this great **CREATION**, with very definite paths laid out from this planet Earth right up to our Spiritual Home, in Paradise, for all serious *Success-seekers* to follow. It also offers *very precise answers* to all serious questions and *definite solutions* to all problems concerning human life here on this Earth and in the whole of Creation. And *that* really gives every one of us the *joyful assurance* of finding his own right way upwards, by the Grace of the **Almighty LORD**.

And so it naturally happens that, before the keen inner eyes of the *genuine* and *serious* seeker of the **Light** and **Truth,** the right ***Way***, the ***Purest Surest Path*** of True Lasting **SUCCESS** in life, stands quite unmistakably glaring! If one really very *diligently strives* to picture it to himself, *within himself*, by *carefully* and *conscientiously* following the *high guidance* that is given to him therein. In the **GRAIL MESSAGE**, by **Abd-ru-shin**!

NOW, with so much abundant and truly inexhaustible wealth of *Spiritual Revelations or Teachings* available to all of us on this planet Earth, right now, we must very urgently and resolutely get started! By striving to fully and *meticulously* absorb these *illuminating resources.* That is, very clearly, correctly and completely, towards our personal *spiritual advancement.* I must also acknowledge and include here, on *a very personal* and *totally private individual level,* something else. And *that* is, any new and authentic revelations from on high that may come down to any *earnestly seeking, open-minded person* at quite opportune and *solemn* moments are *meant for his own personal use only!*

For the Almighty **KING**, our **GOD**, is neither *absent* nor *silent* at all, but very *graciously* inclines and reveals His Living Word, *His Light of Truth,* from time to time, to all those who are seriously longing, with a pure heart, to establish a sacred link or *reverential connection* with Him. For such truly is the ever-consistent *Loving Grace* of our Heavenly **FATHER**. Therefore, my fellow *Success-seeker,* faithfully *Ask, Seek and Knock,* in truly *fervent, childlike and humble supplication*, for His divine help, and you will surely *never* be disappointed! Exactly in accordance with the sacred *Promissory Advice* of the Great CHRIST, **JESUS**, *"Ask, and you shall receive!"*... *"Seek, and you shall find!"*... *"Knock,* and it *shall be opened unto you!"*

It is precisely the constant, *faithful* practice of this great *Christ Advice* and the resultant benefits gained thereby that actually enable us to truly recognise our Great **MAKER**, His **Holy Will** and **Great Love** much more clearly. And it is then through these sure recognitions that we are able always to consciously, confidently, and joyfully be, live and work diligently in our individual lives, *exactly according to* His *ALL-WISE,* **HOLY WILL**. NOW, towards this realisation, one must start with the spiritual *cognitions* absorbed from the *authentic resources* at one's disposal to strive further for *true recognition* via very keen *real-life* practical applications. That is, by meticulous testing and probing, all backed, of course, by constant, very humble supplication for divine support.

And it is most likely then that one will be able to turn his recognitions into *solid, steady* and *vital Conviction.* The *Absolute Unshakable Certainty* which indeed is the very sure *mainspring* and *mainstay* of that *ever-victorious* spiritual *power, Faith…* **Holy Faith!** The great instant *Power, Sword* and *Shield* of *Victorious Working* and *Combat,* in and by the **WORD** of the **LORD!** *This* is exactly what we always need for the *unavoidable Battle* against the *Darkness* here on Earth and in this whole world! We actually need it for bravely facing and overcoming the opposition, the obstacles and malicious attacks of Lucifer's hateful minions or agents out here.

Holy Faith! It is *truly* the essential **Power** that we always need for our conscious and confident, courageous and thereby triumphant journey along the **GREAT SUCCESS HIGHWAY**. It is indeed the *sure* **Key** to the gate of the Kingdom of the **LORD**, Whose great and *irresistible* **POWER** very *protectingly* surrounds any *faithful Success-seeker* who bears within himself the *holy, Unshakable* **Conviction** and **Trust** in that divine *Help* as a *condition.* In addition to all this, one must constantly strive to *actualise* and *perfect* the *Unique Meaning* of his own Being in order to be *exactly what* and *who* one is really meant to be while also diligently performing his specific *personally recognised Roles, Responsibilities* and *Duties* which very precisely constitute for him, the *Prime Essential Purpose* of his conscious existence.

And *all this* must be in *strict accordance* with the Absolutely Perfect, All-Wise Holy Will of the **Almighty LORD**, Which **alone, absolutely alone**, ensures one's **True Lasting SUCCESS** in this life. Therefore, with regards to this great *Attainment*, **True Lasting SUCCESS**, all that I can do here, as a fellow *Success-seeker* and *an ordinary-level, LifeLong Apprentice* of the **Living WORD of the LORD** *myself*, is *only to share* with you and, **neither to convince nor teach you at all**, *what* I have been able to absorb, through my personal real-life *experiential learning process* hitherto. And if you are *now* ready, then allow the **'Great Quest'** to begin! Let it begin with *very bold* and *cheerful enthusiasm*. No *doubt,* no *distrust,* no *fear,* and no *timidity!* Just like a *Success-seeker* who is strongly inwardly driven and motivated by the *inspiring words* of that truly great English luminary, **William Shakespeare**, who in one of his wonderful literary works, a very long time ago said:

"He deserves to have, who knows 'The Best and Surest WAY' to get!"

And in this very context, ***The Best and Surest WAY***, dear fellow *seeker,* is truly:

'The GREAT SUCCESS HIGHWAY'... 'The Principled WAY of the MOST HIGH!'

Which indeed is the **'Purest Surest PATH'** Of **True Lasting SUCCESS!**

IT IS with great pleasure indeed that I present to you, next, a brief **Poetic Prologue**, with a *Fervent Prayer* that you will *surely find* the **'True Lasting SUCCESS'** you are *ardently* seeking, through your own *diligent use of it.* **Amen!**

THE PROLOGUE

GREAT SUCCESS HIGHWAY!
Is the 'Principled WAY!'
The MOST HIGH portrays
To seekers of 'The WAY!'

In the WORD of the LORD
Surely lies 'The WAY!'
The seeker must find
That will him convey!

Listen to the LORD
Of all the Worlds!
Obey His WORD
And 'The WAY!' is yours!

IGNORE the world!
BUT stay on 'The WAY!'
For ways of the crowd
Always lead astray!

SUCCESS that stays
Is found in the Rays
The WORD radiates
Unto him that prays!

Stand Firmly in its Light
And therein strive aright!
With all of your might
Sternly avoid the night! #

GREAT SUCCESS HIGHWAY!
Is the 'Purest Surest WAY!'
The MOST HIGH Portrays!
To him that supplicates!

May we all find It – 3ce.
Amen! Amen!! Amen!!!

 # *the night* is... the Darkness!

SPECIAL ACKNOWLEDGEMENT

ALL Praise, Jubilant Gratitude, Honour and Glory belong *entirely* to the ***Great* LORD!** The **Almighty CREATOR**. WHO *Absolutely Alone* is the **SOURCE** and **SUSTAINER** of all Being, all Life, of all *authentic* Knowledge and Wisdom. The Primordial **ORIGIN,** of *All-embracing* **POWER,** which creates, animates, maintains and sustains, and furthers all things, processes, activities, movements and development towards fulfilment and perfection of all that exists in this great **CREATION!**

By His **Holy Light Power, Creative Will,** He brought all of us into existence and thence continually *illuminates* our Hearts and Minds, our Intuition and Conscience, such that, through consciously and humbly opening ourselves up to His Divine *All-wise Guidance* and *great Leadership,* we can very clearly, correctly and completely *recognise* our *unique individual* and *collective* **Meaning**. And also the *Prime Essential* **Purpose** of our Conscious Life; as *human spiritual,* childlike *part-bearers, pioneers* and *dispensers* of His **Holy Light**, Which embraces His **Truth, Love, Justice** and **Purity,** His **Wisdom** and **Power**. Also, His **Peace** and **Joy,** as well as Natural **Beauty,** with its very essential uplifting element, **Harmony!** All for the attainment of true *Welfare, Progress, Prosperity* and *Supreme Joy, plus the Blissful Ascent* of all mankind, here on Earth and in the whole of this wonderful **CREATION**. In very strict accordance with His **Holy Almighty Will**.

It is *only* through those *guided* *recognitions that we are able to find and follow our *exact* individual ways of *Self-development* towards the *divinely ordained Actualisation* and *Perfection* of our *Being*, which is then characterised by full *Self-consciousness, Maturity, Absolutely Free Will, Power, Active Intuition* with *Balanced Conscience and Nobility*. All of which are needed by us for *spiritually being* and *living* a corresponding *lifestyle*, plus working aright and *effectively* down here. And for being always *prepared* and *ready* to *fight ethically*, for whatever is really *good* and *just* whenever it is necessary, *but…* strictly *without wanton violence, devastation* or deliberately *harming* our fellow men, causing them *misery*, *pain* and *suffering* in the process, just to satisfy our own *selfish desires!*

Thus, every one of us who *seriously* desires True **SUCCESS** *with Lasting Benefits* in this Life, *must* constantly and consistently strive to perform his *personally recognised* Roles, Responsibilities and Duties, so *diligently* that he is thereby able to *actualise* and *perfect* the **Unique Meaning** of his *Being*. And to thereby also *achieve* those ^**High Life Goals** that precisely constitute the true *essence* of the **Prime Essential Purpose** of his own conscious existence. *Which* is to *be, live* and *work aright*, joyfully, gratefully, in very strict accordance with the Holy Almighty Will of the Absolute **LORD** of all realms, our **GOD**, in all eternity!

<u>High Life Goals</u> comprise thorough (*i.e., very Clear, Correct* and *Complete*) Knowledge of:
1. This Great **Creation** of the **MOST-HIGH**, to which we all belong, as *parts* of it!;

2. His **All-Wise Holy Will** and its *Automatic Executives*, **CUE Laws**, *operating* therein!;

3. The **MOST-HIGH** Himself, *as far as it is really possible; for we can never see* **Him**!;

4. An *earnest volition* and *efforts* to joyfully diligently *co-operate* with *like-minded* others for the actual transformation of this *planet Earth* into a *glorious* **Kingdom of the Almighty GOD**, in absolutely *Loyal Devotion* to **HIM** *alone!* In *humble* and *happy* **Obedience** to His 'Supreme LAW'; "I... AM THE LORD! Thy GOD! Thou *Must Not Have* Any Other Gods But ME!" An *absolutely imperative* **Divine ORDER**, which very directly authoritatively demands an *all-exclusive, humble,* and *total submission* from all of His *human spiritual creatures*! Which *must* thus be promptly acted upon, through serious and holy fulfilment of the *Very Solemn Vow,* **'Thy Kingdom come! Thy Will Be Done On Earth, As It Is In Heaven!'** Borne by **'The LORD'S PRAYER'**, the **SUPREME COVENANT** that was most lovingly given to us here on Earth by the CHRIST, **JESUS**, for our **Salvation, Redemption and... Blissful Ascent!**; and

5. Developing thereby a *true Childlike Connection* in an *intimate* **Bond** of *Pure Reverential and Selfless* **Love** for **HIM!** In fulfilment of the *closely corresponding* **'Supreme LAW Of LOVE'**, also most graciously given to us, earthly humanity, by The Christ **JESUS**, **"Thou Must Love The LORD, Thy GOD, With *All* Thy Heart, *All* Thy Mind, And *All* Thy Soul!".**

EXCEEDINGLY GREAT, MOST HOLY AND TRULY *WORTHY* INDEED... IS... THE ALMIGHTY **LORD!**

OF... OUR *FAITHFUL* **E**XALTATION,... *SOLEMN* **A**CKNOWLEDGEMENT AND... *DEEP* **R**EVERENCE.

OF *SACRED JUBILANT* PRAISE AND *HEARTFELT* GRATITUDE.

All... IN *PURE, SELFLESS,... REVERENTIAL* **LOVE** FOR **HIM!**

WITH... OUR *WHOLE BEING, LIFESTYLE,... AND VOCATION,...* IN ALL ETERNITY!

AND SO BE IT!

PART 1: *True* SUCCESS

Fellow *Success-seeker!* To begin with, I wish to ask you a very crucial question. What exactly does the *concept* of **SUCCESS** mean to you? Really? I ask you this question because, as you may very well know already, every one of us has his own personal conception of this very significant and popular *phenomenon,* either clearly or vaguely borne in mind. By my asking this question, I seek to draw your attention unto this important matter and prompt some *reflection* on it before going further into details. For an important question such as this one always helps one to immediately achieve a sharp focus and to start probing, searching within, and thereby becoming receptive to the inflow, into one's mind, of possible answers and *pictures,* which are more or less directly related to the specific *object* of that question!

Very many and quite diverse indeed are the definitions or conceptions of **SUCCESS**, which are borne in mind and held out by many of us today. And when, out of my keen interest and the wish to broaden the scope of my own cognition of this very important concept, I ventured to check out the exact *meaning* two of the popular commonly used English Dictionaries had to offer, the list of diverse and *thought-provoking* conceptions given below was the outcome:

Issue, favourable result, good fortune, prosperity, something that succeeds, the end or object desired, the accomplishment of an aim or purpose, the gaining of fame, wealth or social status, a person or thing that succeeds.

Now, going by the diversity of conceptions, both from the above list and generally, one can quite easily perceive that this very word **SUCCESS** definitely means different things to different people. Thereby, one can also very easily ascertain the various *yardsticks* by which it is measured and affirmed by different individuals or diverse groups concerned. A very common category of those *yardsticks* is defined mainly in materialistic terms, invariably consisting of tangible earthly possessions like *money*, houses, cars, clothes, shoes, jewellery, lucrative businesses, etc. To that very transient category of earthly *material symbols* also belong things like earthly position, position power and influence, connections, social esteem or fame and comfortable lifestyle. There are also others, like contentment and happiness.

And in light of all these, there is also a particular opinion that *only* a balanced hold of all the above-stated yardsticks can serve as genuine proof of True **SUCCESS** in this life on Earth. Also, one can occasionally hear or read of the opinion that those people who possess these apparent signs of prosperity are in that position because they are quite *definitely* in the good books of the **ALMIGHTY**. That the **MOST HIGH** has blessed them so graciously with these possessions as a *reward* for the good quality of their particular being, lifestyle, and work on Earth! Probably you too, fellow *seeker*, must have heard it sometimes said that this or that apparently wealthy person is a *big Man or Woman* and as such is definitely a real *Success!*

And all this appraisal is usually based upon the outwardly perceived social status, huge earthly material possessions, and maybe also a grand lifestyle.

All of these opinions are, however, based *entirely* on our
own human *value judgement systems* down here on Earth.
Now, if one takes into consideration the diversity of opinions existing about the concept of *True* **SUCCESS**, it is
very tempting indeed to simply assume or jump to the
conclusion that we are dealing here with a *relative phenomenon*. This means that it can simply be defined and
authenticated by means of any or all of our various ideas
about its true nature, and also that it is thus *dependent* on
how each one of us sees or makes it for himself. But really, does it? Absolutely no! The *reality* is not so at all! For
True **SUCCESS,** that is *Real Prosperity*, on this Earth, in
this world and in the whole great Creation of our **LORD**,
is strictly a very *inherently consistent Phenomenon*.

This means that the exact *Criteria* by which it *must* be attained and the *Specific Standards* of *Evaluation* by which it
is verified and affirmed, lie steadfastly anchored within
itself alone! And this assertion stems from the fact that
True **SUCCESS** in this life is very much *all-exclusively based
upon* and *enabled* by the divine **CUE LAWS** of the **LORD**,
which are the exact *natural expressions* and *automatic
executes* of His Holy WILL here on Earth and in all the
worlds. Thus, the ***Absolute POWER, AUTHORITY*** and
RIGHTS to *judge, verify and affirm* the true **SUCCESS** of
all His human spiritual creatures, *in this His own Creation*,
belong to Him absolutely *alone!* Or who else has that supreme and all-embracing *Wisdom* to accurately judge the

being, *lifestyle* and *activity* of a *human spirit*, on this Earth, in this world? And then, to affirm authoritatively that he has correctly *actualised* and *perfected* his true *meaning* and thereby also fulfilled the *prime essential purpose* of his conscious existence here?

WHO else but the All-Wise, Almighty **LORD** of all the worlds? For the *specific* appraisal of true **SUCCESS** in this life (i.e., its real evaluation) is naturally executed by the divine **CUE LAWS** of the great **CREATOR** *alone!* It means, therefore, that He and absolutely He alone, can most accurately judge and affirm a human being's true **SUCCESS** in this life and nobody else! Thus, *in this very regard*, all of our human measures and standards of assessment down here have no validity or any merit at all! And so also is any human declaration or pronouncement which may be made thereby. For hardly or very rarely do any of our own perceptions, ideas, thoughts, opinions or wishes regarding the real *meaning* and exact *purpose* of human life here on Earth, or in this world, coincide in any way or form with the **CUE** Laws, Commandments, and thereby with the All-wise, Holy Will and divine Judgement of the Almighty **LORD!**

Therefore, *none* of our human accomplishments, which we very often praise and like to celebrate with great pride here on Earth, can ever count as True **SUCCESS** before the **LORD**, *unless* they strictly accord with His divine Laws and Commandments and thus with His Holy WILL and *Evaluation or Judgement Standards.* Thus, no matter how great it may seem to us, there is none of our human achievements down here that may be described as true

SUCCESS *unless* its nature and form, plus, most especially, the ways of its attainment, very accurately match the ordained operational standards of the divine Laws of the Almighty **LORD**, the **Supreme AUTHOR** of all life!

Very far removed from it also are all those human achievements that are based upon the *ignoble principle* which asserts that *'The end justifies the means!'* Since all of these types are focused mainly on the earthly outcomes, without any due regard whatever to the basic ethical principles of the Laws of the **ALMIGHTY**. Not to speak at all of any consideration for the human rights, wellbeing, peace of mind, progress, prosperity, joy or happiness of others. This very kind must, of course, eventually lead to great sorrow and perdition for all those that are involved! Now, in order to further affirm the *exclusive* Divine Authority of the Almighty **CREATOR** over this very important matter, let us now take the time to examine the following illustration.

Today, we all know the fact, for instance, that it is *only* the *manufacturer* of an electronic gadget, such as a mobile phone or a laptop computer, who has *conceived* its research, design and development, plus the fabrication and operational processes, who actually holds all *ownership rights* over it, for he is also the one who has set up the technical data and performance standards for his own product. In addition, he also lays down the quality assurance and performance appraisal procedures. He then makes adequate provisions for its maintenance in order to sustain its service life in the field. Right? Is it then true or not that such a manufacturer who has an all-round knowledge of his own product is understandably the best judge over it? Also, is he not the *sole authority* who can justifiably declare that his own product, the real child of his own brain, is ultimately either a *success* or *failure* in the field? Verily, verily, he is!

Now, we can similarly say exactly the same as regards the absolute Power, Authority and the Rights of judgement held by the Almighty **CREATOR** over all of us, His earthly *human spiritual creatures*. Or can we not? Of course, we can most logically draw that conclusion! That the Almighty **LORD** *alone* is the Sole **AUTHORITY** Who can rightfully judge and affirm either the true **SUCCESS** or *utter failure* of any human being in this life on Earth and elsewhere in His own Creation.

For by virtue of His express divine Creative Volition: **"Let Us make man in *Our Own Image,* after *Our Likeness!*"** (Holy Bible, Genesis 1:26), HE alone knew and still knows precisely what that **image of His Likeness**, its real *meaning* and the exact purpose of existence must be! As the ***sole* AUTHOR** and **MAKER** of man's life, the great **LORD** is thus the *only rightful* **JUDGE** over him and the quality of life that he has led hitherto, that he is leading now or may lead in the future. With that undisputable fact established, we, His *human creatures*, have no other sensible option *right now* than to humbly strive to learn from Him what really is His own divine *concept* of *true* **SUCCESS** regarding our lives and activities in this great Creation that is His alone! We must acknowledge and also never forget the fact that the Almighty **CREATOR** already had very clear and most accurate pictures, in His Sacred Mind, of what kinds of human creatures He thus wished to make, and for what purpose, when He said, **"Let Us make man *in Our Own Image*, after *Our Likeness!*"** That is, in the likeness of ***Our Own Image!***

There is no truly *faithful* person who could doubt this fact or expect anything less than this *absolute clarity of divine intention* from the **MOST HIGH**, the All-Wise! He knew very well the exact kind of human creatures that He wished to make and exactly for what purpose! We must therefore strive to learn from Him the correct attainment method, and *evaluation process* of this highly significant *Value.* It follows then that any one of us who is seriously seeking *True Lasting* **SUCCESS** in his own life here must diligently perform that very important duty, *personally* and *directly* for his own benefit, through his fervent, childlike and humble supplication for divine help of the necessary instruction, guidance and leadership. Each person has to earnestly seek a very clear understanding of the real *meaning of his own being* and the exact *purpose* of his existence upon this Earth now, and generally in this great Creation. It is so very unfortunate and sad indeed that, going by the present general conditions on this planet Earth, a great majority of us *appear* to have no interest in this highly significant *quest* at all!

We tend usually to guess at it or even leave that task for others to perform for us, or we just simply copy others. Who quite often include the so-called *social role models* upon the basis of some perceived and admired earthly advantages which they seem to enjoy at the current time. And *that...* is wrong! Very wrong! My fellow *seeker,* please take note that these words are only intended to raise a very crucial issue of very *high significance* so that you may take the acquisition of this *very essential knowledge* seriously. I am *not myself at all better or higher* than any other person in this regard. *First*, I am very much one of us, and *second*, it took me quite a long time to actually begin to realise how so very serious, so *highly significant* and utterly *indispensable* this *essential knowledge* is for me, and I am still learning, continually! And surely, there is a very bright light at the end of the tunnel, since *"He who asks, receives!" "He who seeks, finds!" and "Unto him who knocks, the gate is opened!"*, according to the words of *sacred assurance* of the Christ, **JESUS**.

Thus, I hereby urge you, as a fellow *success-seeker* and ***not teacher or expert at all***, to take this matter *very seriously* and not allow yourself to be led astray or deceived by anyone about its very high significance and utmost urgency. FOR the understanding which you thereby *personally, independently,* seek and gain will form a *very reliable basis* for all that you may henceforth decide to do towards the attainment of your own True Lasting **SUCCESS** in this life. Indeed, we can all benefit greatly from the loving advice of the Christ, **JESUS**, regarding man's *prime essential purpose* of life, by which we are all meant to bear within us and spread the Light of the **MOST HIGH** around us down here on Earth and in the whole world:

*"You are the **Light** of this world! A **lamp** is not lit just to be hidden under the table, but placed on top of it for all in the room to see by it." "So, let your **Light** so shine that when*

*men see by it, they will give glory to your **Father Who is in Heaven!**"*

With this we can grasp the fact that we are all made to *be, live* and *work* aright down here as human spiritual *part-bearers* of the **Light** of our Great **MAKER**, for the benefit of all humanity and the entire CREATION, in His Honour. For this purpose, the **ALMIGHTY LORD** has blessed each one of us with many *pure* and *great potentialities*, that is, latent powers or abilities, which we were meant to promptly awaken and diligently develop into full *executive powers* that we all need for the glorious fulfilment of the *prime essential purpose* of our conscious existence in this life. *That* is precisely through the competent and effective performance of our *personally* and *correctly* recognised specific *Roles, Responsibilities* and *Duties,* which are firmly linked directly to that essential *life purpose,* in exact accordance with the Holy Will of our great **CREATOR**. And *that,* actually, is the real essence of True Lasting **SUCCESS,** which all genuine *Success-seekers* down here are striving for. Now, let us move on to examine this great ***Phenomenon*** with due earnestness and strive to *clearly* and *correctly grasp* its defining factors so that we can thereby ensure *lasting benefits* for ourselves through their correct, diligent application.

'TRUE SUCCESS is an *eternal process* of gradually and diligently *actualising* and *perfecting* the *unique meaning* of one's *Being,* and thereby progressively attaining the *High Life Goals,* which most certainly constitute the *Prime Essential Purpose* of one's conscious life. In *exact accordance* with the All-Wise, Holy Will of the **ALMIGHTY**.

BUT, *very strictly* without *deliberately harming, disturbing or hindering the welfare, progress, prosperity and peace of* one's fellow men, or even *daring to violate* their *natural rights* in any way or form in the process**!'**

A very careful and thorough examination of this statement is quite capable of leading one to conclude that the attainment of *True, Lasting* **SUCCESS** in this life *cannot be easy* at all. And why is that? First, like everything else which is really good in this world, True **SUCCESS** is not and cannot be easy or cheap to attain, at all! For starters, there are very many high standards and targets to meet, plus numerous tough challenges to overcome on the way, in the bid to *attain* and *sustain* it. Above all, the *fact* that its *attainment criteria* are so *firmly linked* to and *strictly enforced* by the Holy Creative Will of the Almighty **LORD**, thus by His **CUE LAWS of Creation** and **Ten Commandments**, that they all make very serious demands on the *Success-seeker,* quite logically lends due credence to that conclusion.

This *fact* being as it is, there is, however, the very good news that it is indeed very much achievable! And *that* is because the **ALMIGHTY LORD**, out of His Great Love, had already most graciously made abundant, absolutely inexhaustible provision of all things that we will ever require for our *being, living* and *working* aright down here, in order for us to achieve True Lasting **SUCCESS** in this life. The *right way* to the discovery of all those gifts is very clearly shown to us in this His **Creation** to which we all belong and in **His** Living **WORD.** Therefore, all that we *must do now* is to seriously strive to absorb His Living **Word** *aright* and then very humbly adjust ourselves to His *all-wise* Guidance contained therein for us. This comes up in the forms of His perfect **CUE LAWS** and **The Ten Commandments**. We are surely the ones who *must now* seriously strive to follow His divine Guidance and Leadership in the proper way that is required of us, so that we can really *succeed* in this life.

NOW, since the *concept* of True **SUCCESS** is deeply and very strictly rooted in the Holy Will of the **MOST HIGH**, as indicated earlier on, it is important that we undertake a careful examination of its *Key Defining Factors*, the basic and *imperative Standards* of its *Attainment* and *Evaluation*. This exercise helps one to very correctly grasp the real meaning of the *concept* and to thereby make the right *self-attunement* to it, in such a manner that unfailingly guarantees the desired happy outcomes. Those Standards are presented in the following list:

1. **An *Eternal Process.***
2. Gradual, diligent ***actualising*** of the ***Unique Meaning*** of one's *Being.*
3. Gradual, diligent ***perfecting*** of the ***unique Meaning*** of one's *Being.*
4. Progressive ***attainment*** of ***High Life Goals***, which directly constitute the ***Prime Essential Purpose*** of one's Conscious Existence.
5. Very ***Strict Accordance*** with the **All-wise, Holy Will** of the **ALMIGHTY LORD**.
6. **Without *Deliberately Harming, Disturbing*** or ***Hindering*** *the welfare*, progress, prosperity and peace of one's fellow men or even *During to* **Violate** their *Natural Rights* in the Process.

The degree of one's *earnest* learning and *careful* and *conscientious* application of these *basic standards* in one's life and activity will *directly influence* one's possibility or not of attaining the desired *True* **SUCCESS** with *lasting benefits.* Let us therefore strive to grasp them aright in order to ensure correct and fruitful practice.

1. ***An Eternal Process.***

A very apt saying goes: *'True* **SUCCESS** *is a **journey**, and not a destination!'* Thus, an intrinsic characteristic and distinctive qualification of True **SUCCESS** is that it is not at all a *one-off accomplishment*, but ***A lifelong Process!*** This notion helps the serious *Success-seeker* to immediately and very clearly grasp within himself what he is actually about, and to thereby also be fully prepared for the *endless diligent activity* that is thus required of him from the very start of his quest. Readily accepting this so *unavoidable* challenge, plus the realisation that the serious seeker's paths always hold gracious support from above, makes it easier for one to firmly adopt and exercise the requisite *trustful faith, cheerful courage* and *unswerving focus* all the way. And *that* helps greatly!

2. Gradual, diligent ***actualising*** of the ***Unique Meaning*** of one's *Being.*

Regarding this *Standard*, what is very important to hold in mind always is the very *urgent necessity* for one to really know himself very clearly, correctly and completely, whereby one can then strive with all one's might to be exactly his own *true self* at all times. *Very much easier said than done!* For the strong volition of a *Success-seeker* to *actualise* the *Unique Meaning* of his own *Being* will quite automatically awaken in him the questions, *'What am I?'* and *'Who am I?'* And the correct answers must be found because it is not possible to *actualise or develop* something that one does not really know or understand. The first question here is seeking to discover the basic *essential meaning* of one's being, aiming to grasp the real *essence* of oneself, which in our own case is *spiritual!* We are all *human spiritual creatures* of the **ALMIGHTY CREATOR**!

The second wishes to discover the *functional meaning* of one's being, that is, to unveil one's *precise vocation,* which naturally embraces his *specific* roles, responsibilities and duties here on Earth and in this great Creation. These two aspects of a person's *unique meaning* naturally combine to characterise him as a *unique* human spiritual personality here on Earth for a *definite function* and in *exact accordance* with the Holy Will of the Almighty **CREATOR**. Now, having identified the *essential* aspect of the *unique meaning* of a human being as *spiritual,* the *functional meaning* then also has to be clarified. And it is very *exciting* indeed to realise that the latter is very deeply rooted in the *Name* of a person. It is contained in the very *Name* that a person bears down here, which as such urgently needs to be very thoroughly understood by its bearer, who then has to very promptly awaken and develop its real *concept* to full executive power. For every *Name* is a *word* that naturally bears some sacred living power within it, plus the very *specific indication,* guidance, of what exactly its bearer is here on Earth to do now (i.e., what his definite *personal vocation* in this Earth life really is).

The *Name* is, in fact, a *natural bundle* of certain characteristics, traits, abilities or talents which its bearer is here on Earth to manifest, to develop and express, or refine further for diligent fulfilment of the *prime essential purpose* of his own conscious life. Exactly in accordance with the Holy Creative Will of the **ALMIGHTY**, who brought him into life here on Earth and in this Creation. Now, having grasped aright both aspects of the *unique meaning* of one's being, the next step is to strive most diligently to *actualise it* (i.e., to make it as *real* as it is meant to be), and as much as possible. This begins with one's striving resolutely for his own spiritual awakening so as to become truly *spiritual,* as one's *essential meaning* dictates. It is then naturally followed by very keen efforts to ascertain one's specific life roles, responsibilities and duties which truly accord with the *functional meaning* that is indicated by one's *Name*!

IT IS very important here to emphasise the *great significance* of *fervent, childlike* and *humble supplication* to the Almighty **LORD** for His divine guidance in this matter. For without His help, it is absolutely *impossible* to find clarity. But whenever this need is properly attended to, the outcomes are very rewarding indeed. And It is through this occurrence that a keen and careful observer can recognise the *Name* in its bearer and his activity, which then makes him say: *'Aha! The saying is very true indeed!' 'That the Name actually influences its bearer!'* Quite synonymous with *"By their fruits ye shall know them!"* *'Their fruits'* in this context meaning *'Their perceived manner of being and lifestyle, plus their work or activity',* which all naturally flow outward visibly and tangibly from the power of the *Name* of the person concerned. For the *Name* indeed naturally motivates, constantly and consistently impels its *bearer*, always driving him, to carry out those deeds which naturally accord with his true *meaning* and *purpose* in life!

Hence through the way and manner in which the person who is *conscious* of his own *Name* is just *being, behaving* or *comporting* himself, and also diligently performing his specific *roles, responsibilities* and duties, he must quite unavoidably *actualise* his two personal aspects. These are the *essential* and *functional* aspects of the *unique meaning* of his own *Being or Personality.* This is the crucial stage of one's development when one becomes inwardly aware of some strong promptings that keep on urging him to pursue a certain relevant activity. He now knows himself clearly and thereby goes on consciously and confidently *being* and *living* as his own real self while also joyfully *working* along his personally well-recognised paths! And thereby, he is in the right state to apply the third factor as well.

3. Gradual, diligent **perfecting** of the **Unique Meaning** of one's *Being.*

In the clear consciousness that **True SUCCESS** is an *eternal process,* the *Success-seeker* knows that there *cannot* and *must not* be a slackening of his efforts anymore. The constant *inner urge* to undertake the gradual, diligent *perfecting* of the *Unique Meaning* of one's *Being,* which then persists, is in fact a call to engage oneself in the process of *Continuous Personal Development for Excellence.* That is, to always strive towards becoming the *very best*, *highest* and the *greatest* of oneself that one can ever possibly be. In the firm knowledge of the *fact* that the Almighty **CREATOR**, our **LORD,** strictly demands perfection of *Being, Living and Doing* from every one of his human spiritual creatures! *"Become ye therefore perfect, as your heavenly* **FATHER** *is perfect!"* says the Christ **JESUS**. And *not* to adopt at all, in any way or form, a *self-degrading* or *depreciating* lifestyle whereby one *very unfortunately* adopts an *unholy comparison* of oneself with others, who are naturally completely different personalities of their own.

Not even to entertain within oneself, a rather socially prevalent but pitiful *'greater-than, lesser* than' *or 'higher-than, lower-than'* inner attitude, which will thereby make one a *despicable caricature* of other people who indeed naturally have completely different *personal meaning* and *purpose* of their own! Because this condition can very easily cause one to lose personal focus and sense of direction in life, we must strive at all costs to avoid it! The gradual, diligent ***perfecting*** of the **Unique Meaning** of one's *Being* that we are striving for in this quest is very firmly aimed at constant enhancement or elevation of the *spiritualised* state of one's being, lifestyle and vocational activity. And this, however, also involves the crucial need to *collaborate effectively* at times with other *kindred* or truly *like-minded* people. Those who genuinely share *similar values* in life and are also able and keen to cooperate peacefully and harmoniously with oneself in the execution of some *similarly* and *clearly* recognised beneficial activities that will bring real blessings to the partners, as well as fellow human beings in general.

A very important fact *again,* is that the gradual, diligent *perfecting* of the *Unique Meaning* of one's *Being* here on Earth, in this great world, cannot be done effectively at all without the divine help of the Almighty **CREATOR**, as it is the case with all serious endeavours. And it is very helpful to remember that we are not alone in this quest, for the gracious Help of our **Great LORD** is always around us, and all we need to do here is to humbly supplicate to Him for it. Thus, with the sacred, unshaken trust that we will surely receive it, the strength we need to strive onward triumphantly will be given to us. And it is through this *Pure Faith Approach* to *Self-realisation* that the serious *success-seeker* must always try to firmly align his personal volition with the *Divine Volition*, Holy Will, of the **MOST HIGH**, who will then surely facilitate one's fulfilment of the Prime Essential Purpose of life in this Creation.

4. Fulfilling the ***Prime Essential Purpose*** of one's Conscious Existence.

Now, hand in hand with the correct, *faithful* application of the third *Standard* given above goes this one. This achievement is, in fact, the direct outcome of the diligent efforts made to achieve the relevant *High Life Goals* referred to earlier on in the statement of the *Special Acknowledgement.* It actually comes along as the *Success-seeker* proceeds on diligently performing his *personally recognised* specific roles, responsibilities and duties, which are very firmly linked to those *High Life Goals.* What exactly are those *High Life Goals?* And why are they qualified as *High?* These are very significant, *highly essential spiritual values*, which, on that account, really deserve to be called *High Life Goals*, in very strict contrast to all earthly accomplishments.

They are also the *fundamentals* of the *Prime Essential Purpose* of man's life, in exact accordance with the All-Wise, Holy Creative Will of the **ALMIGHTY**. The **very first** *High Life Goal* is the clear and correct grasp of the *true knowledge* of this great Creation to which we belong, to really grasp its multi-dimensional nature and structure. For the Almighty **CREATOR** communicates daily and directly to all of us through His living Creation, via the natural manifestations of His absolutely pure and perfect **CUE Laws,** which directly execute His Holy Will everywhere around us. Since one is an intrinsic *particle* of this great Creation, it is therefore important to really strive to grasp the clear, correct, and complete knowledge of it together with those of the *absolutely incorruptible* Laws which are operating therein. And this *true knowledge* is what actually helps one to know how exactly to *be, live, work* and *travel* about therein in a *lawful, harmonious, peaceful* and *joyful* way, in exact accordance with the Holy Will of our Great **LORD**.

The **second** *High Life Goal* is firmly connected to and indeed derives from the first one. It demands from us human beings the *thorough knowledge* of the absolutely perfect **Holy Will** of the **MOST HIGH**, by Which He reigns supreme over all that be and live in the whole great Creation, as the Absolute Almighty **RULER.** Again, this very essential knowledge of the **Holy Will** is, in turn, made possible *only* through the correct knowledge of the

CUE LAWS, which are **its** *natural expressions* and *automatic executives*. These **CUE LAWS** are operational throughout the whole Creation, constantly forming and animating, motivating, maintaining, sustaining and furthering all forms of life within it, including us human beings.

By their collective activity, they lead, guide and help us to be, live and work aright in accordance with the All-wise Will of the **LORD**, in order that we may thereby achieve True **SUCCESS** with lasting benefits in this life. That is, in as much as we willingly and humbly strive to adjust our own volition to them by seriously striving to learn, know and humbly follow their guidance. In fact, without them and their furthering help, we human beings are completely lost and are *neither* able to really *actualise* and *perfect* the unique meaning of our being nor are we able to really fulfil the *Prime Essential Purpose* of our conscious existence at all. Therefore, we *must* very earnestly diligently work to attune ourselves completely to them, both inwardly and outwardly, which is exactly the same as *complete* and *humble* submission to the Holy Will of the Almighty **LORD**.

The **third** *High Life Goal* in this logical sequence is the clear recognition of the sublime Being of the Almighty **CREATOR**, which naturally develops through one's very clear and correct knowledge of and total humble self-submission to His Holy Will, for it is indeed through the genuine wish and diligent efforts to humbly submit oneself to His Holy Will, that the truly wonderful *real-life personal experiencing* of His *divine Attributes* begins. This *personal inner experiencing* is what then gradually develops into a very *unshakable conviction* of His *Reality!* Those *divine Attributes* of the **ALMIGHTY**, which very visibly and tangibly convince the *Success-seeker* of the *absolute reality* of His Being, include His great Love, Justice and Wisdom, plus His All-embracing Power. IN FACT, it is not possible at all for a person to *wholeheartedly love* the **LORD** and to surrender himself fully to Him as such without *first* acquiring an *unshakable conviction* of His existence and sublime Greatness, which manifests through these Attributes. For one will otherwise only be *faking* it then, in blatant and fatal *hypocrisy*!

But, with the *genuine conviction* that comes out of one's *inner experiencing* of His divine Attributes and the deep inner sensing of a *sacred connection* to Him that is awakened thereby, an even greater longing to get ever closer to Him then arises within one. This stage is the **fourth** *High Life Goal*, whereby one is genuinely motivated to ever be, live and work strictly in accordance with His All-wise, Holy Will, in pure reverential love for Him. This is the greatest and the most uplifting attainment that a human being can ever achieve in life, and it is the source of the greatest joy in a person's entire life as well. *But it does not come so easily at all!* And this is because of our old habits, which tend to stand in the way of progress in this regard! This naturally very achievable *High Life Goal* quite firmly demands a very serious, really honest, exclusively good-willing resolution from any one of us who wishes to attain it. And this is exactly the same for all *High Life Goals*. Again, a very pure, serious, sincere and very strong volition that is backed with fervent, childlike and truly humble supplication for the divine grace of the

Great **LORD** will surely yield the desired outcome, eventually. For the Almighty **CREATOR**, our **LORD** is **LOVE**!

The **fifth** *High Life Goal,* which naturally develops from all of the above-listed ones, in a logical sequence, is the exercise of an earnest volition and efforts to unite with *like-minded people*, kindred spirits, to strive most diligently and vigorously for the glorious establishment of an earthly **Kingdom of God** down here! In absolutely loyal devotion to Him, all-exclusively *alone*! Which admits none other than the all-exclusive reign of the **Almighty LORD** as the *Sole RULER* of all realms of existence, in all eternity. This corresponds directly to and is synonymous with humble obedience to the **Supreme LAW of the LORD, "I... AM THE LORD!... Thy GOD!... Thou *Must Not Have* Any Other Gods... But ME!"** And at the same time, it constitutes the fulfilment of the sacred vow, **'Thy Kingdom Come!... Thy Will Be Done On Earth As It Is Done In Heaven!'** which is contained in **'THE LORD'S PRAYER', The Supreme Covenant**, that was given to us, *earthly humanity*, as a great divine help towards the attainment of real salvation, redemption and joyful ascent to the pure luminous Kingdom of **GOD** above, Paradise.

5. In ***Strict Accordance*** with the ***Holy Creative Will*** of the **ALMIGHTY!**

As already hinted above, we can immediately sense the fact that *being, living and doing* in strict accordance with the Holy Creative Will of the **ALMIGHTY** presupposes *correct* prior knowledge of that Holy Will. Without *this,* we are at a loss as to how really to adjust ourselves to It in all aspects of our lives. Therefore, we have first to very clearly and correctly grasp its *natural expressions* and *automatic executives*, thus the **CUE LAWS**. Because the divine Will naturally manifests itself by these **LAWS.** But not these alone! We also need to self-adjust to the ***Ten Commandments*** of the **LORD**, which fully and precisely *explain* and *Interpret* for *practical purposes* this great Will for us all to follow. Thus, the two sets of divine Laws must be taken together and very clearly, correctly, and fully grasped and strictly obeyed by us at all times. For this exactly is what *being, living,* and *working strictly in accordance* with the Holy Will of the **LORD** demands. And it is *only* via this humble *strict obedience* that we are always *supported* and *enabled* to firmly, strongly and securely plant our feet upon the Great **SUCCESS HIGHWAY!**

6. **Without *Deliberately Harming*, *Disturbing*** or ***Hindering*** *the welfare*, progress, prosperity and peace of one's fellow men or even *Daring to* **Violate** their *Natural Rights* in the Process.

The *Key Point* here, very simply, is to employ the great power of true **Love**! Everyone who seriously seeks True, Lasting **SUCCESS** in this life most unavoidably needs this *extremely powerful force* as the greatest support ever in order to ensure permanent prosperity for himself in this life! Here, the *golden advice* of the Christ, **JESUS**, very sharply comes into focus with an absolutely *imperative* demand:

"Love Thy Neighbour as Thy Self!" And with that also goes another, which quite firmly states: **"Do to Others**

as You Would Like Them To Do to You!" These two highly significant, admonitory calls from **JESUS**, the CHRIST, quite simply contain all that we must seriously heed if we genuinely desire True Lasting **SUCCESS** in this life. To listen to them and resolve to obey them, fulfil them to the letter, always means we can never contemplate the need to deliberately harm, disturb or hinder a fellow human being in any way or form, just in order to satisfy our own desires. Most especially when we are striving to achieve True **SUCCESS** with Lasting Benefits. It will also never occur to us to *dare wilfully* to *violate* the natural rights of our fellow human beings for the same reasons.

For we must always remember that "Whatever we sow in this regard will most certainly return to us, *in multiple measures*, when the *time of due harvest* comes around!" And that there is *absolutely no escape* from this utterly inflexible Law. Therefore, the only *sure way or safeguard* here is **Love,... True Love!** Which can very simply be defined as:

'Absolutely *Pure, Perfect* and *Consistent, Wholehearted, Wholeminded* and *All-embracing Selfless Goodwill!'*

This particular **Seven Star** *definition* speaks for itself, and I honestly believe it needs no further explanation. What remains for me and you is to decide to earnestly adopt and put it into constant practice. For **Love** is Indeed the *highest,* the *greatest* and the *most powerful* gift of the Almighty **CREATOR** that a human being can ever receive and also give or express towards his fellow men! And you know what? This greatest of all values is eternal and inexhaustible, and thus, everything it truly deeply touches cannot but bear *true lasting values*. That is, prosper abundantly and perpetually unless it is fouled up through some evil, unclean, or unjust and even selfish acts. On sober reflection upon the current state of human affairs here on this planet Earth, however, one can quite easily perceive the fact that **True Love** is in very short supply indeed. For we can very visibly and tangibly perceive all around us, on an almost daily basis, the ugly effects of man's *negative* and *violent vibrations* of *hatred, the direct opposite* of real **Love**, that constantly *manifests through anger and aggression, bitterness, envy* and escalating incidents of violence, wars, murders and destruction, etc., everywhere and almost every day on this planet Earth! And all this is surely *a CALL* for us to wake up!

A CALL for us to resolutely act fast, *in good time*, and change the dangerous, deadly pattern of life that has been prevailing hitherto down here, before it is too late to really secure our salvation and simultaneously to stop desecrating this planet Earth, our temporary station. This means that we must all take very serious steps to bring back **True Love** into our human life and interactions down here, in such a way that will really enable us to make a very firm and strong link with the **Great Fountain of True LOVE** above such that we can be helped soon enough to *victoriously* stride forward and upward again. As was the case a very, very long time ago, before the very *woeful* and *lamentable failure* which occasioned the pitiful *downfall* of our own humanity out here!

Once again, **True Love** is the very best, highest, the greatest and the most powerful gift from our Heavenly **FATHER** to us. Genuinely bearing it within oneself and really living in it always, in an *absolutely unselfish way,* will greatly help us to advance forward and also upward in an *unstoppable* manner while at the same time enabling us to gain the most essential *Value* in life. *THAT* is an intimate and greatly uplifting relationship with the Almighty **LORD**, which is the *happiest* attainment for every serious *success-seeker* in this life. For it truly belongs to and comes solely from the **MOST HIGH,** Who Himself is **LOVE**, Absolute **LOVE!** The *only* true **BESTOWER** of all lasting Blessings!

Finally, in order to be able to achieve all these very lofty goals of life, one has, first and foremost, to have a genuine and serious willingness that is bent on attaining them. And all it takes really is to firmly back one's volition with heartfelt and humble supplication for the divine Help of the **LORD**, the All-Wise! Since no one else has the *Power* and the *Wisdom* to help, lead and guide us in this quest. And while firmly bearing that highly significant need in mind, let us now move on to carefully examine the concept of the **Supreme LAW of the LORD!**

PART 2: The SUPREME LAW of the LORD! – One And Only *Mainspring* and *Mainstay!*

In the preceding part 1 of this book, we have learned that we can achieve *true* **SUCCESS** with lasting benefits *only* by striving for it in strict accordance with the All-Wise Holy Will of the **LORD.** This is an absolutely and eternally *irrevocable condition* that demands that we must diligently learn, correctly know its **CUE LAWS** and fully adjust our entire life to them. For they not only naturally express but also automatically execute that Holly Will in this Creation. And it is *only* in this way that we can receive the help and support needed for our *Success-seeking* efforts. We will look into the nature and joint activity of these **CUE LAWS** more closely in part 3 of this book. But right now, we need first and foremost to carefully examine the very special, fundamental and highly significant **LAW of our LORD** as a matter of *utmost necessity* and *urgency*. It very clearly, directly and quite authoritatively *asserts* and imperatively *demands:*

"I… AM THE LORD! THY GOD! THOU *MUST NOT HAVE* ANY OTHER GODS… BUT ME!"

THIS… is the First of the **TEN COMMANDMENTS OF GOD,** which He sent down to us through the great Prophet **MOSES** about three and a half thousand years ago. You may then ask, *'Why the great urgency today or now?'* Well, the real answer is this: The **Ten Commandments of GOD** are indeed the true and detailed *Explanation,* as well as the very practical *Interpretation* of His Holy Will for us human beings down here. And by virtue of their inherent stern *Moral Principles*, they provide all of us with the most reliable *advice* and *guidance,* which make it really possible and safe for every one of us to rightly adjust himself to the Holy Will of the Almighty **LORD.**

Now, the very first of these Commandments, stated above, is precisely the *holiest,* the *highest* and the *most sublime* of all Commandments or Laws of our great **MAKER!** This is precisely why the CHRIST, **JESUS** Himself, called it the **SUPREME LAW of the MOST HIGH** while He was down here on Earth, on His great Mission of Salvation. And guess what? This sublime **LAW,** *in its essence,* actually predates the event of the Primordial Creative Command, also known as the **LAW of Creation**, *"Let There Be Light!"* by which this great Creation to which we all belong was brought into existence. Very irrefutable is the fact that the **ALMIGHTY CREATOR** was, eternally before this Creation, as He is right now and will forever remain unto all eternity, the *absolute* and all-exclusive **LORD** of *all realms of existence* and… **GOD!**

Thus, the **SUPREME LAW of the LORD** naturally stands out *distinctly* among all other divine Laws and serves as a mark of *His Sublime Majesty,* which thereby justifies its being qualified as the **SUPREME LAW of the LORD**! Very remarkably also, this Law is the *only* one of His **Ten Commandments** by which He speaks personally directly to us, His own *human spiritual creatures,* indicating thereby how exactly we must regard and relate to HIM personally! And He thus very *authoritatively* and *justifiably* demands a humble and *all-exclusive* reverential worship, thus absolutely unalloyed self-devotion and service to Himself alone! Hence:

"THOU *MUST NOT HAVE* ANY OTHER GODS… BUT ME!"

The absolutely irrefutable fact is that we all completely depend upon this humble self-submission to this **Supreme LAW of the LORD** for our welfare, the attainment of our full self-consciousness, maturity, nobility, prosperity and ascent in this life. It is strictly, absolutely *inviolable* and so must never be broken in any way or form by any one of us. That is, anyone who is really serious about attaining True Lasting **SUCCESS** in this life. There is, in fact, no other Law in this CREATION by which we are so sternly commanded to strive for true knowledge of our great **CREATOR,** together with how appropriately we must relate to Him, than by this **Supreme LAW**. However, it is very important indeed to emphasise here that one's humble obedience to this **Supreme LAW** *must* also be extended to the other nine Commandments of the **LORD** with equal seriousness.

Since they all belong to and have come to us from Him, there is no other option for us than to embrace all of them and thereby prove our genuine respect and honour to Him. More importantly, they altogether teach us how really to be, live, think, speak and work aright, with regards to His Holy Will, in order to really prosper and thereby be truly at peace and enjoy *lasting* supreme happiness in life. Now, since our true **SUCCESS** in this life absolutely depends upon our *strict obedience* to all of these **Commandments of the LORD**, it is very important indeed that we must begin *right now* to make very serious efforts to carefully *grasp them aright*, as a matter of great urgent significance. To enable us to put them into good practice, constantly and consistently, in all aspects of our being, lifestyle and activity.

Fellow *Success-seeker*, please find below a list of these very special **LAWS**, the **Ten Commandments of GOD, our LORD**, the wording of Which may appear rather strange to you because they are herein stated differently from the usual presentation that we all have hitherto been accustomed to. The *new compelling tone* of these **Commandments** actually stems from the *fact* that we are *now* definitely living in the foretold *End Time*. The time of the *Last Judgement*, of the *Great Purification* of all mankind and the world, which had been prophesied a long, long time ago through the divine messages which the **LORD** had sent down to us over the past eras. These are now the days of the *Last Judgement* of us all by the *Executive Justice, the Holy Spirit, Holy Will* of the **Almighty CREATOR**.

We all now live in that time when each one of us *must* clearly prove how he or she really stands regarding all of His divine **LAWS**, His Holy Will and thereby, before **HIM**. For or against? In full accord and humble submission or *obstinate disregard* and *conceited opposition?* Whereby, in exact accordance with how each one really stands, he earns for himself true lasting **SUCCESS** with supreme peace and happiness, plus the most glorious gift of eternal life in the pure luminous Kingdom above, or utter failure that leads to eternal damnation. NOW, whereas with regards to these *special* **LAWS**, we have hitherto been used to the words ***'Thou Shall'*** and ***'Thou Shall Not'***, we are all now faced by the *imperative*, most *compelling*, **'Thou Must!'** and **'Thou Must Not!'** And thus, do I also feel compelled to present these great **LAWS** as follows:

The First Commandment:

I... **AM THE LORD! THY GOD!** THOU ***MUST NOT HAVE*** ANY OTHER GODS... **BUT ME!**

The Second Commandment:

THOU ***MUST NOT*** TAKE THE **NAME OF THE LORD**, **THY GOD** IN VAIN!

The Third Commandment:

THOU ***MUST*** KEEP THE SABBATH DAY HOLY!

The Fourth Commandment:

THOU ***MUST*** HONOUR FATHER AND MOTHER!

The Fifth Commandment:

THOU ***MUST NOT*** KILL!

The Sixth Commandment:

THOU **MUST NOT** COMMIT ADULTERY!

The Seventh Commandment:

THOU **MUST NOT** STEAL!

The Eighth Commandment:

THOU **MUST NOT** BEAR FALSE WITNESS AGAINST THY NEIGHBOUR!

The Ninth Commandment:

THOU **MUST NOT** LUST AFTER THY NEIGHBOUR'S WIFE!

The Tenth Commandment:

THOU **MUST NOT** COVET THY NEIGHBOUR'S HOUSE, NOR HIS FARM, NOR HIS CATTLE, NOR ANYTHING THAT IS HIS!

And now comes the *Big Challenge!* Simply memorising this list will not be of any benefit to any of us at all. They must be absorbed in their full details and taken together as one integral body of The **LAW of The LORD**. For they very clearly explain and interpret His **HOLY WILL** for all of us in practical terms. Very strictly, it is *'All or Nothing!'* And as such, we have to make them the **solid**

foundation of our entire being, lifestyle and work, always. And if we earnestly act accordingly, we will surely prosper! Fellow traveller, I trust that you have grasped the real core, *main thrust*, of this matter by now.

In all earnestness, the fact that it is our Great **CREATOR** Who is addressing each one of us directly through those great LAWS, most especially the *First one*, is very much *enough motivation!* It is truly enough *motivation* for every serious seeker of *Permanent Prosperity* in his life to humbly respond to them in total *reverential obedience.* For thereby one cannot fail to clearly perceive, through the ensuing personal experiencing, that the stated **Supreme LAW of the LORD**, the highest, holiest and greatest of all divine Laws, is the *surest* MAINSPRING and MAINSTAY of real wellbeing, progress and lasting *Prosperity* in this life.

Quite significantly, again, it just happens to be the *only one* that is so distinctly and uniquely personal, as a *direct address* from the **ALMIGHTY LORD** to the individual *human spiritual creature* down here on Earth. Very *justifiably* stern, it authoritatively asserts and imperatively demands:

"I... **AM THE LORD! Thy GOD!** THOU ***MUST NOT HAVE*** ANY OTHER GODS... **BUT ME!"**

Which is why I wish hereby to say to you, *fellow seeker*, that if you are really keen on absorbing this prime Commandment of the **MOST HIGH**, together with the other nine, *as an integral whole*, in their comprehensive forms, for the *truly great promise* and high *values* that they hold ready for all genuine seekers, then you should promptly strive to obtain the great Work that is titled:

THE TEN COMMANDMENTS OF GOD AND **THE LORD'S PRAYER** BY **ABD-RU-SHIN** – ISBN 1-898853-10-X

The contents surely promise truly *joyful experiences* and *lifelong gains* for anyone who earnestly strives to absorb and diligently put them to good use as advised therein. And if one backs this personal activity up with the very necessary *fervent, childlike* and *humble supplication* to the **LORD** for His divine Help, so that one may be able to grasp the true meaning (i.e., the exact significance, the right sense plus the real purpose of every living concept therein), the glorious enlightenment that results is as truly wonderful as it is very uplifting. According to one's inner state of pure, serious longing and openness, this will surely happen, and thereby the seeker will personally ascertain for himself that he is actually dealing with the real Source of those divine **LAWS**; and that they were sent to him directly from on High for his own wellbeing, progress, prosperity and joyful ascent in this life.

Thereby everyone can surely confirm to himself the verity of the promise, *"Ask and you shall receive. Seek and you shall find. Knock and it shall be opened unto you!"* that was given to us by the great *Truth-Bringer,* **JESUS** the Christ, about two thousand years ago. It is only through one's personal experience that the absolute verity of this loving *Christ promise* can be confirmed. NOW let us go back to the First Commandment of **GOD the FATHER**, which the **CHRIST** referred to as the **SUPREME LAW OF THE**

LORD, and examine it further in order to deepen and expand our perception of it. You see, it is my strong conviction that it was and still is in order to help us to perceive more correctly the very *high significance* and *great urgency* of the need for us to diligently absorb and very humbly submit to this **SUPREME LAW** that He also *very purposely* went ahead to present to us in the context of Pure **LOVE**, whereby He gave us the **SUPREME LAW OF LOVE**!:

"THOU *MUST* LOVE THE LORD, THY GOD, *WITH ALL* THY HEART, *ALL* THY SOUL AND *ALL* THY MIND!"

In reality, by *re-emphasising* the **SUPREME LAW of the LORD** in this new, Pure-**LOVE** context, the **CHRIST** automatically *elevated* its already very high *Value* and *Significance* to an even greater and higher level for all of us. And by doing this, He simply reaffirmed His *earnest assertion* that:

"He did not come to annul His FATHER's LAWS but to fulfil them!"

This sacred assertion is clearly verified by the use of *the same Key Concepts* at the heart of the original **LAW**, thus: **"The LORD thy GOD."** In addition, the stern demand for an *all-exclusive Devotion* of the faithful human being to the Almighty **LORD**, which the original **LAW** makes: ***"Thou Must Not Have Any Other Gods!"*** is reaffirmed in the latter by using the word *'All'* thrice in it. For whoever earnestly devotes himself with ***All*** of his Heart, ***All*** of his Soul and ***All*** of his Mind, thus completely in pure reverential and *selfless Love* to the Almighty **LORD**, exactly as the Christ advised, shows thereby that he has *totally* done away with **'Any other gods'**. Thus, there is absolutely no room or space in his Heart, Soul and Mind at all for any other idols! This is exactly what the preceding **SUPREME LAW of THE LORD** very sternly demands of every one of us!

So, fellow *success-seeker*, the most important thing now is that if we seriously desire to attain True Lasting **SUCCESS** in this life, we must *most diligently* strive to very *clearly, correctly* and *fully* absorb the **SUPREME LAW of the LORD** and *very humbly* obey it at all times! And by doing so, we are indeed also obeying the **SUPREME LAW of LOVE,** which was given by the CHRIST, and which demands exactly the same *all-exclusive self-devotion* to the **MOST HIGH**, just as the **SUPREME LAW** does. Therefore, every *success-seeker* needs to completely and humbly adjust himself to this **SUPREME LAW of The LORD** in order to obtain the desired *lasting benefits* in this life. None of us can really prosper here on this Earth, in this world and in the entire great Creation unless this *highest* and *holiest*, indeed the *greatest* of all commandments, is strictly and fully adhered to. And if we supplicate fervently for the divine help of the **LORD**, so that we can surely receive the strength for its glorious fulfilment, we shall have it. For *"Ask and you shall receive!"* – **JESUS CHRIST.**

PART 3: The Pure and Perfect CUE LAWS of the LORD – *The Sole Enablers!*

In the preceding *part two* of this book, we have explored the very great concept of the **Supreme LAW of the LORD** and have thereby obtained the knowledge of its very high *significance* for all those people who seriously desire true lasting **SUCCESS** in this life. Now is the time to view the **CUE LAWS of the LORD**, the *Sole Enablers* of true Lasting **SUCCESS**, which most accurately express and automatically execute His Holy Creative Will **"Let There Be Light!"**, by which this great CREATION was brought into existence. These **CUE LAWS** are the true helpers for all serious *Success-seekers* who always diligently strive to adjust their whole being, lifestyle and vocation to the **Supreme LAW of the LORD**, which is the main driving force at the core of His Holy Creative Will.

For the **ALMIGHTY** was indeed the Absolute **LORD** and **GOD** of all great *Existence*, even before He willed this wonderful Creation into being, just exactly as He is at this very moment and remains for all eternity! The absolute significance and very irrefutable necessity of these **CUE LAWS** imply that we must promptly and earnestly heed them if we truly wish to achieve anything of real value down here, live in real peace and be happy. Because they are the *Sole Enablers* of all manifestations (i.e., all processes and activities, and fulfilments of life events in the whole of this Creation, unto all eternity, as ordained by the Almighty **LORD**!). Thus, any one of us who seriously desires to really *permanently* prosper in his own life must very diligently strive to learn and know aright and *humbly adjust* himself to these **CUE LAWS** completely!

NOW, the word **CUE,** which qualifies these **LAWS**, is mainly an *acronym* for their natural characteristics. The first letter, **C**, stands for *Constantly-Consistent*, which affirms the *unswerving regularity* of individual and joint activity of these natural **LAWS!** The second letter, **U**, simply means *Universally-Uniform*. A confirmation of the very steady *uniformity* of their operation in all universes of this great Creation. From which reality the saying *'As above, so down below!'* has arisen. And the last letter, **E**, stands for *Eternally Exact and Exacting!* Clearly portraying the *absolute precision, flawless accuracy* and the utterly *irresistible force* with which these **LAWS** always operate, everywhere, in exact accordance with the very perfect nature of the Holy Creative Will of the Almighty **LORD**, which they altogether precisely express and automatically execute!

So, the word **CUE** simply portrays the *unstoppable* and *unchangeable* nature of these **LAWS of the LORD**! By their adamant characteristics, they very sternly urge every genuine *Success-seeker* to always take a very serious and firm *cue* from them. That means we must constantly strive to learn, know and obey them *very strictly* by acting exactly as demanded of us without reservation! Now, since these **CUE LAWS** are the executive arms of the Holy Creative Will of our **LORD**, we have to build our requisite knowledge of them upon the *foundation* of the accurate knowledge of the *Holy Creative Will* itself.

We know already that it was by this *Creative Will* that the Almighty **CREATOR** brought this great Creation into life, plus ourselves eventually! Very marvellous indeed are the *biblical pictures* of the events of that great *process*!

NOW, with the very deep insights provided in the great Spiritual Work of **Abd-ru-shin**, **'In The Light of TRUTH – The Grail Message'**, it is possible to *inwardly perceive* that process as clearly and correctly as one can. Thereby, one can *visualise* how, by the pronouncement of the Creative Command, ***"Let There Be Light!"***, enormous waves of the all-embracing creative power of the **LORD** promptly shot out from the divine, *eternal realm* of His Holy Light Radiations into the hitherto totally *empty* and *dark* spaces that were on the outside. And just from those powerful waves of the *Living Light* came into existence all that is now collectively known as Creation. Including our world, with this temporary station that we currently live upon, the Earth. That great Primordial Creative Command or Holy Creative Will, **"Let There Be Light!"** can be explained or interpreted simply as follows:

'**LET THERE BE** *strictly Luminous* and *Dynamic, Lawful* and *Beautiful* manifestations of Light (i.e., *Life*, by constant, consistent and harmonious movements, and thereby development towards *perfection* of all that are brought into existence by this *Primordial Creative Command*). Very firmly upon the basis of true Love, Justice and Purity of the great CREATOR, who *alone* ensures total wellbeing, peace, progress, prosperity, supreme joy and blissful *ascent* for all His creatures. Absolutely in His honour and glory *alone* unto all eternity!'

***PLEASE** take very careful note here that this statement is my own personal perception of the Creative Command! I am very conscious of the fact that you may get a different perspective of the Command to the one given here when you prayerfully reflect deeply upon it by yourself, for yourself, as it is naturally demanded of every one of us.*

In any case, authentic concepts will surely arise within you, which will confirm that your very own perception and the one presented here have come from the same Source! And for that very reason they will vibrate in harmony. Let us, therefore, stop here for a short while and reflect upon the contents of the above statement carefully. HERE we do have some clearly stated *standards* upon which anyone who seriously wishes to learn and obey this Creative Will can base his whole life activities. Four very significant qualitative standards for the accurate fulfilment of the *Creative Command* lie in the first sentence. There we have the words **luminous** *and* **dynamic**, **lawful** *and* **beautiful!** These are meant to show us very clearly how the nature of our own fulfilment of the Holy Creative Will of the **MOST HIGH** must be.

First of all, *the prime standard* **luminous** demands of us that the conscious exercise of our *free will power*, in our intuitions and conscience, our thoughts, speech and visible physical deeds should all be **luminous** and thus be totally free from all darkness! Since all that is dark is against the Will of our **CREATOR.** The second standard, **dynamic**, demands constant, consistent and harmonious activity from all of us who wish to really obey the Holy Will here on Earth and in the whole great Creation.

In reality, this utmost *dynamism*, spiritually and physically, is a very strict and inviolable requirement for our development and real fulfilment in this Creation, exactly as ordained by the **ALMIGHTY**! The third standard, ***lawful***, calls for an attitude of total *compliance* with all of the natural **CUE LAWS** of the divine Creative Will of the **LORD** in all things and all circumstances of our life.

To be included here also are the *Ten Commandments* of **GOD the FATHER**, which constitute the *authentic Explanation* and *practical Interpretation* of His Holy Will for all of us here in His Creation. The fourth standard, ***beautiful***, demands that we must always strive to ensure real beauty in absolutely all things because earnest fulfilment of the Creative Command, **"Let There Be Light"** cannot be without real beauty. Since the Holy Light of the great **LORD** unavoidably bears real natural beauty within It. Indeed, they are absolutely and inseparably one! Such that Light is Beauty, and true Beauty is Light! It is therefore very important, at this point, to state the *seven defining principles* of true *natural beauty*, which I found in the **WORD** of the **LORD**, and which every one of us can diligently master and joyfully apply as a guide for himself, in ensuring the ordained *true natural beauty*, in all aspects of his own life, as a *part-bearer* of the **Light**.

True Natural Beauty! A very essential quality of Living Light! its first principle that must be observed in all things is ***purity***. This strictly calls for keeping things as natural and simple as ordained by the **LORD**. Thus, clean and completely undistorted. The next one is ***orderliness***! This demands the perfect logical arrangement of things in a very simple, uncomplicated manner, which thereby enhances efficiency and effectiveness! There is also **balanced coordination**, which demands the bringing *together* of things that are truly *compatible* or similar and making them *operate and* work *together* smoothly in such a way that assures *perfect equilibrium* as well as enabling **functional integrity**, another principle, to manifest. And with the latter naturally emerges the fifth principle, **harmony!** The natural state whereby all parts or members of the whole really vibrate *pleasantly* or *joyfully* together and in *unison*, perfect attunement to the sacred rhythm of the natural vibrations of the **Holy Will** of the **ALMIGHTY**, the **LIGHT**!

This is what again allows *noble* forms to arise in a truly dignified and *graceful* manner, thereby further revealing two very important qualitative principles of true *natural beauty*: **dignified nobility** and **gracefulness!** We see here that the fourth *operational standard* of the Holy Creative Command of the **LORD** is defined by seven qualitative principles! **Purity, Orderliness, Balanced Coordination** and **Functional Integrity, Harmony, Dignified Nobility, and Gracefulness!** And with regard to the seventh principle, **gracefulness**, it is a fact that whatever is truly **graceful** is, as such, also elegant, possessing attractive and therefore pleasant qualities. It always awakens a vibrant sense of true joy within the observer, who is able to perceive its real essence.

Indeed, the foregoing explanation shows clearly that this natural value, **True Natural Beauty**, comes from above. It is an intrinsic characteristic of the activity of the **CUE LAWS,** which execute the **Holy Creative Will** of the **ALMIGHTY**, **"Let There Be Light!".**

Let us now return to those four qualitative standards given earlier on as ***luminous*** *and* ***dynamic***, ***lawful***, *and* ***beautiful***. It is very important for us to seriously take all of them together and diligently work in and with them through every act of our personal free *Will* **Power**. Via our *Intuition* and *Conscience*, our *Thought*, *Speech*, and visible physical *Deeds*. Thereby also in the performance of our specific personally recognised Roles, Responsibilities, and Duties, by which one can really *actualise* and *perfect* the *unique meaning* of his *Being* and also fulfil the *prime essential purpose* of his conscious existence in this life. BUT there is still more! If we go back to view the statement of the *Primordial Creative Command* that is given above, we find even much more *imperative standards*, the careful observation of which will further assure our progress upon the great **SUCCESS HIGHWAY**.

Those are given in the words **Constant**, **Consistent** and **Harmonious**, which must unitedly qualify the nature of our conscious activities as we seek to fulfil the Will of our **MAKER** while we are at the same time developing towards the ordained perfection of our being. It is very important here also to be very mindful of the *most significant factor*, the *greatest* and the *most powerful* force which actually drives all things up to glorious fruition in this life, and *that* is the *True* **LOVE** of the **Almighty LORD**. This highest, most benevolent *Value* alive is the greatest gift of our **LORD** and must, therefore, be taken by us as the firm basis for all of our striving, in a totally *selfless manner,* in order to *ensure* our true and permanent **Prosperity** in this life!

With that said, let us now examine the **CUE LAWS** of the **LORD**, which naturally jointly express and automatically *execute* His Holy Creative WILL, **"LET THERE BE LIGHT!"**, and which are the *Sole Enablers* of True Lasting **SUCCESS.** So very significant are they for our true **SUCCESS** in life that we must seriously strive to grasp them aright. Very clearly, correctly, and completely and then try to fully adjust ourselves to them as diligently as possible.

1. The CUE LAW of NATURAL LUMINOSITY

"LET THERE BE LIGHT!" In the *Beginning*, when the Almighty **CREATOR**, the **LORD** our **GOD**, wished, out of His great Love, to bring this wonderful Creation into existence, He pronounced the *Primordial Creative Command,* **"Let There Be Light!"** and there was **Light**! According to the biblical accounts of that great happening, the great **LORD** then looked at the outcome of His Divine Creative Act, and He saw that *it was good!* As good exactly, *perfectly,* as He ordained it to be, will be the most logical and absolutely correct conclusion about that. Since the Almighty **CREATOR**, Who Himself is absolutely perfect in every way, could never have brought or would never bring anything that is imperfect into existence.

Now, all human spiritual creatures of the great **CREATOR** are supposed to be, to live and work down here, in this world, as active *spiritual part-bearers* and pioneers of His

Holy Light. Exactly as the words of **JESUS** the Christ affirmed: *"You are the light of this world!"* This was and is intended to awaken or remind and motivate us human spirits of this world to embrace a lifestyle that is filled with pure inner *luminosity* down here. Thus, we must always strive to shine the Light of our great **MAKER**, which we all bear within us outwardly for the good of our earthly humanity and environments.

Therefore, strict obedience to this **CUE LAW Of Our LORD**, by consciously cultivating and expanding our inner Light and resolutely avoiding all that is dark, base, unethical, evil and unlawful, will definitely help us to guarantee our own true lasting **SUCCESS** in this life!

2. **The CUE LAW of MOTION**

"LET There Be Light!" The **Source of Life, Living Light**, cannot but *radiate* or send out its luminous rays vibratingly, in an orderly and beautiful way, for the fulfilment of the divine purpose! Hand in hand with the manifestation of the **CUE LAW of NATURAL LUMINOSITY** also came into action another, which is **The CUE LAW of MOTION**, in strict fulfilment of the *Primordial Creative Command* **"Let There Be Light!"**. This was not only intended to bring this great Creation into existence but also to *animate, drive, maintain, sustain, further* and *govern* all manifestations therein eternally. By that, the *continuity* of existence, of life, as ordained by the Great **CREATOR** was and is forever assured through perpetual constant and consistent movement and real development towards the perfection of all that be!

To ensure that *Continuity*, the **CUE LAW of MOTION** also instantly came into operation. Thus, the *relevant* life event, which also automatically happened under the pressure of the Holy Light Power of the **LORD**, His Creative Command, was this natural **LAW** of Impelled *Motion!* Embracing a very powerful movement of *life essences*, driven by the great force of this Creative Power of the **LORD**! This was and still is the great force of the Holy Light Power within and behind absolutely all manifestations, processes, activities, movements and development in this great Creation, which can only happen through *motion*, exactly as ordained by the Great **CREATOR**!

And since this *motion* is a natural basic sign of existence or life, it also follows *truly* that wherever there is no sign of *motion* or movement (i.e., activity, be it only of infinitesimal dimension), there is no life either! It is indeed the activity of this very **CUE LAW**, which always strictly demands constant, consistent, and harmonious motion and *activity* in perfect alignment with the sacred rhythm of the Holy Will of the **MOST HIGH**. It is important to state that the manifestation of this particular **CUE LAW** also called forth the operation of the other **CUE LAWS**, *together* with which it then naturally continued and still steadily continues to cooperate in the constant maintenance and sustainance, furtherance and *governance* of this great CREATION!

NOW, since we human spirits of this Earth are also parts of this great Creation, we must constantly endeavour to strictly obey this **CUE LAW of MOTION** by being always active or mobile, spiritually and physically, in order to remain alive, healthy, strong and happy therein. In reality, this is how we truly obey the Holy Creative Will of the Almighty **LORD**, who demands constant, consistent and harmonious joyful activity, in complete and most humble adjustment to His **CUE LAWS**, from all of us. Whereby the voluntary happy compliance with that sacred demand will surely have an uplifting effect upon us. We can have a glimpse into this effect from the following portrayal of the beneficial activity of the next **CUE LAW** on any person who positively adjusts himself to it.

3. **The CUE Law of NATURAL GRAVITATION**

"LET There Be Light!" In the fulfilment of this *Primordial Creative Command* whereby *impelled motion* naturally occurred as described above, the **CUE Law of Natural Gravitation** simultaneously and unavoidably came into action. Through this event, powerful waves of *vital substances* that were being driven *downward* and out of the divine realm into the outer spaces *on this side of existence* were of extremely high temperatures due to the exceedingly great driving pressure of the Holy Light Power of the Almighty **CREATOR**. As these *vital substances* were pushed *downward*, further away from the SOURCE of all Life, the great pressure acting upon them thereby progressively became less; with the continual increase in distance, their degree of *heat* also began to fall gradually. As the accounts from the *spiritual work* **'In The Light Of Truth – The Grail Message'** by **Abd-ru-shin** reveal.

With this gradual fall in the intensity of temperatures also came the progressive but varied condensation of the *vital substances,* which are of different species. That means some elements were cooling off, condensing, and taking on form faster than the others, each type at a height that corresponds precisely to its own particular nature or species and also according to the degree of its density and heaviness or weight. Naturally, that also meant that all the denser and heavier forms had to sink further away from the Primordial SOURCE of Life (i.e., from the Almighty **CREATOR**), while all of the relatively lighter and more luminous ones had to remain at levels that are nearer to Him as much as it was lawfully possible. It is precisely this *natural capacity* of things to move or sink away from the Origin of Life due to their increasing density and weight that is called *Natural Gravity!* This natural effect was and still is the manifestation of the **CUE LAW of Natural Gravitation**, which works in a *vertical sense* in the whole great Creation and is also in very close and perfect working harmony with the **CUE LAW of Motion**.

With the other **CUE LAWS of the LORD**, these two always and consistently cooperate to determine the actual *level* or *height* that a particular creature, for instance a human spirit, attains in this world by virtue of the *nature* and *quality* of his *inner being.* That is precisely according to the natural density, heaviness or weight, and the corresponding luminosity of his soul. It was indeed through this very process that everything created then became stationed at very definite *levels* or *heights* in all parts of this Creation. In such a way that all that is less dense, lighter in weight and more luminous always stands or floats higher above that which is denser, heavier and less luminous. Thus, each of the emergent categories of created forms thereby occupied and still occupies today such a *level* or *height* that corresponds exactly to its natural density, weight and luminosity in the vast Creation! This fact is true for the natural positions, *levels* or *heights* of all cosmic systems and bodies, the planets, the sun, moons and stars known to us today.

Now, it is very worthy of note to state that by virtue of the *Primordial Creative Command*, **"Let There Be Light!"** any part of Creation is *only* able to retain its natural *level*, *height* or *position* therein strictly by striving constantly and consistently to maintain itself in that state. Including, most especially, we human spirits who were and are still expected to start our own development down here because of our *spiritual unconsciousness* and *immaturity,* which made it impossible for us to experience or partake in the very intense real-life activities that prevail in our home base, Paradise. We had to come down to this region of far less pressure in order to be able to begin our very essential but rather slow process of spiritual awakening and development.

Down here, we are able to fulfil this gradual development at a pace that is just right for us. For this, we needed and still need to wear some special material cloaks or bodies as an outer protective covering, which enable us to live down here properly and go through all of our necessary *learning* experiences while developing towards the perfection of our being as divinely ordained for us. It is due to the **CUE LAW of Natural Gravitation** that is acting upon our outer cloaks that we could achieve the necessary *descent* into this material realm for our much-needed *incarnation*, *birth* and gradual development. That, exactly, is how we could travel down here, just by acquiring more density and weight as we put on one covering after another, in one plane after another, until finally we arrived down here on this earthly plane via *incarnation* and ensuing *earthly birth!*

It is also by the effect of this **CUE LAW**, *in the opposite direction*, that we are indeed able to rise upwards again back to our origin after we have completed our growth here on Earth, in this material world, in the proper manner that has been ordained for us by the Almighty **CREATOR**. That is, strictly in accordance with His Holy Will, which then enables our strong and conscious connection to our spiritual home base, Paradise. We can then drop the worldly cloaks or bodies that we have needed down here and freely strive upwards again. But it is not all as easy as it sounds, although it happens quite naturally and simply! What, then, can possibly be in the way? It is the very serious and diligent work that we all must carry out in order to ensure our safe and joyful return to our luminous home again!

We must, therefore, learn, know and diligently be, live and work in exact accordance with the demands of all **CUE LAWS**, thus of the Holy Will of the **LORD**, with special attention to the *exacting activity* of this particular **CUE LAW of Natural Gravitation**.

There is a very urgent need to be fully aware of *how* it can support our *progress* and *ascent*, depending on the proper use of our gift of *free will*. For if we are always careful to use this great gift of our **LORD** all-exclusively *only* for what is truly good, noble, pure and light, the cloaks of our souls are thereby less dense and much lighter in weight and also more luminous. And the downward push or pressure of this powerful **CUE LAW** upon our souls is thus *much* reduced to the extent that we can easily rise upward once we cast off our heavy material body at the right time of physical earthly death. We are then enabled to rise upwards on our homeward journey more easily towards Paradise. This happening is very similar in character to the release of a *helium-filled balloon* from the load or weight that has been holding it down so that it can freely rise aloft! But if we choose to use our *free will power* for what is evil, impure, or dark, the outer cloaks or bodies of our souls become denser, heavier, and thereby darker.

Inevitably, then, this great **CUE LAW** has the effect of pressing, indeed forcing one to move in a downward direction to the dark regions of *hell* and *damnation*. This is a very serious and frightful realisation that should give one strong motivation to always strive to use his *free will* for what is exclusively good and pure, light and noble, as a very sure safeguard against the *woeful downfall!* And the greatest, most effective safeguard here is for one to always strive earnestly to avoid all kinds of *propensity!* **Propensity!** What is that? Simply, it is an excessive and prolonged bad, base, dirty or immoral *habit.* A *bent* inner attitude and or behaviour, which a person has cultivated and sustained in such a way that it thereby *dominates* and *rules* over him always! It tightly binds, controls, and so inescapably enslaves a person to himself that he finds it difficult, if not at all impossible, to free himself from it again without very special help! THERE is nothing that can more definitely hinder or block a person's spiritual growth and ascent in this life than a *propensity* that has been *personally cultivated* or *self-imposed*! Thus, it is very helpful to always remember that:

'*Propensity blocks true prosperity. It* makes *dense* and *deadens* the soul of man!*'

It is, however, very important for us to take note of the fact that the **CUE LAW of Natural Gravitation** is, by nature, *very neutral,* like all the others. It is how we human beings use our *free will power* that dictates the nature, form and direction of its effects upon us, either upward towards the Light or downward into the darkness. And in fact, we all know exactly what makes an evil attitude and behaviour and what is otherwise good. Also, we *can wilfully make a good choice if we really want to,* for we have all been blessed with the great power of morality and *conscience,* in addition to the *free will power.* And for the avoidance of doubt, however, we have to be very clear about the kinds of inner attitudes and behaviours implied herein. These include uncontrolled anger, bitterness and hate, fraud, theft, artifice, deception, malice and murder, greed, avarice, covetousness, envy, rape, incendiarism, bearing false witness, unforgiveness, hypocrisy and, worst of all, the acts of blasphemy and blatant sacrilege against the Holiness of the Almighty LORD, our **CREATOR**!

We are fully, irrevocably responsible for our acts of will, volition, choices or decisions, plus our actions as well as their effects. Knowing that our actions can be intuitive and intellectual or thought, verbal and physically visible deeds and that we have the *powers* to always control all of them, if we really wish to do so, is a very big help! If we earnestly desire this **CUE LAW** to support our upward striving positively, this is the knowledge that helps us to be very *deliberate* and *diligent* in making the right choices or decisions with corresponding actions. We only need to be conscious of the fact that every *evil* act of will surely pulls a person downward while every good act uplifts one. We are thereby always rising and falling through our alternating choices and corresponding actions. It is, therefore, better to be *deliberately consistent* in always choosing only good, exclusively good deeds over evil ones in order to ensure a steady ascent for oneself.

Again, it is a fact that none of us here is either *perfect* or *strong enough to work alone, successfully* in this regard, most especially in view of the constant opposition and the attacks of the *Darkness against* any of us who may seriously resolve to abide by the **CUE LAWS**, the **Commandments** and thus the **Holy Will** of the **ALMIGHTY** always.

And *that* is why we all need constant *fervent, childlike,* and very *humble* supplication for *Divine Help*, as a matter of utmost urgency and necessity.

And if we consistently follow this humble path, we will surely receive the power that will enable us to *triumph* and joyfully stride forward and upward. Once again, the **CUE LAW of Natural Gravitation** never works alone but together with the other **CUE LAWS** to support us. So, let us now move ahead to examine the next one.

4. The CUE LAW of HOMOGENEOUS ATTRACTION

"Let There Be Light!" Another *natural expression* and *automatic executive* of this great *Primordial Creative Command* is the **CUE LAW of Homogeneous Attraction.** Naturally, it manifests as the mutual *pulling effect*, *magnetic action*, of bodies or things that are of exactly the same kind or similar nature upon each other. Therefore, all *homogeneous* species tend to exert upon each other a certain measure of attraction by the force of their mutual *natural magnetism*! While the action of the preceding **CUE LAW** manifests mainly in a vertical sense, up-down or down-up direction, this **CUE LAW** cooperates by acting in horizontal directions at every level, height, or plane in this Creation. Now this means that while the **CUE LAW of Natural Gravitation** is exerting its force on an object either in a downward or upward direction, according to its exact *density* and *weight* at the time, the **CUE LAW of Homogeneous Attraction** collaborates by simultaneously ensuring that it is pulled towards its own exact kind or else that it attracts to itself the other, depending on its strength, precisely at the place or level that corresponds to its *inner nature*.

Now, in the case of us human beings, all this happens strictly as a direct result of what one has determined for himself by the prior use of his *free will power* together with his conscience and the exact nature of his soul, good or evil. This **CUE LAW** ensures that a human spirit will automatically attract and is also attracted by its own similar kind, in its newly attained level, environment or area of existence. The fact that it firmly enforces the coming together of all that is of the same nature is easily perceptible through the constant manifestations of its effects all around us. The popular sayings *'Birds of a feather flock together'*, *'Like father like son'* and *'Show me your friends, and I will tell you who you are'* have all surely arisen from careful observation of the consistent activity and influence of this perfect and changeless **CUE LAW.**

Now, how really can we use this knowledge to our own advantage, ensuring that we can always have truly pleasant, happy experiences in this life? The answer is by the *conscious* and *deliberate* use of our *free will power* for what is exclusively good, just and noble, most especially when it comes to our interpersonal relationships with our fellow men. Thus, by seriously directing our volition or wishes, through our intuition, thought, speech and physical visible deeds towards *only* what will benefit our human as well as material environments! It is in this way that we can generate personal radiations of nature and strength, which are capable of attracting good outcomes towards us.

It is precisely by the way we *use* our *free will power* and *conscience* that we naturally attune ourselves to other prevailing homogeneous radiations at any given time and place. *The choice is ours*, good or bad, luminous or dark, pleasant or unpleasant. Thus, with the careful and correct use of our *free will power* and *conscience*, all exclusively for what is good and just, in strict accordance with the All-Holy Will of the **ALMIGHTY**, we can be absolutely certain that we shall ultimately *attract* and be attracted to nothing else but what is also good and just in this life.

The natural influence of this **CUE LAW** upon the way we use our *free will* power and *conscience* is further made stronger by its joint activity with another great collaborating **LAW**, which is called the **CUE LAW of Automatic Reciprocity** that we are now going to examine next.

5. The CUE LAW of AUTOMATIC RECIPROCITY

"Let There Be Light!" This particular **CUE LAW of the LORD**, otherwise also known as the **LAW of Karma**, **or** the **LAW of Retributive Justice** or else the **LAW of Sowing and Reaping**, is very closely linked to the preceding ones. In all manifestations of the *Holy Creative Will* of the Almighty **LORD**, it plays the role of *adamantly* ensuring that His absolutely perfect and incorruptible *Justice* is strictly and completely enforced. Thereby, it forcefully acts always with absolute accuracy to ensure that every act of *free will* that is carried out by a human being is *automatically* and *precisely* reciprocated. Strictly and most accurately responded to by a reaction of exactly the same nature and effects. The *automatic* effects are very strictly enforced by the inexorable activity of its inherent, *very stern* principles, which were clearly proclaimed to us, earthly humanity, by **Jesus Christ** about two thousand years ago. It will really help us to pay careful attention to those *stern principles* by seriously absorbing and following them so that we can profit from them:

The First Principle: *"Whatsoever a man soweth, shall he reap!"*

Strictly according to the **CUE LAW of Automatic Reciprocity**, this implies that a human being who deliberately acts in a way that brings *suffering* and *pain* to his fellow men will most certainly get the same experience back. On the other hand, if he has given *joy* and *pleasure* to them, he will surely get the same kind back, eventually. Thus, this principle forcibly ensures that we most unavoidably get back exactly *what* we give to our fellow men or release into Creation by the deliberate use of our *free will power* with absolutely perfect accuracy.

The Second Principle: *"As a man sows shall he reap!"*

While the first principle deals with the *exact essence or nature* of an act of will, this one deals with the *way or manner* in which an action is carried out. For example, a *cunning* or deceptive act will unfailingly attract the same manner back to the doer at the end. But an honest action will strictly bring honesty back to one. Again, a *hostile* attitude towards one's fellow men will surely attract hostility back, while a truly *friendly, respectful* and *considerate* style cannot fail to yield exactly the same kind in return.

This means that the *how* of an act of will is equally as important as its *what*! Thus, it demands that we must always seriously consider, beforehand, the way or manner of our approach in dealing with our fellow men. Because these will very surely dictate *exactly how* the effects we must reap back will manifest when these are due. Very surely, *"as we sow must we reap"* in the end! And that *end* is the *exact time* or season of *due harvest!* The next Principle:

The Third Principle: *"At the exact due harvest time shall man reap whatever he has sown!"*

As a very well-known *biblical* saying clearly affirms, *"There is a time and a season for everything under the sun!"* Thus, there is a time to sow the seeds and also a time to harvest the fruits of those seeds! This is the Principle of *'due harvest time!'* It means that man *must* reap the outcomes of whatever he has done, by the exercise of his *free will power* or volition, via his intuition and conscience, his thoughts, speech and also physical visible deeds, as the original *seeds*, precisely at the *exact time of due harvest.*

Absolutely in strict accordance with the very just activity of the **CUE LAW of Automatic Reciprocity**, in the fulfilment of the perfect Holy Will of the great **LORD!** Whenever the *exact time* of reaping the fruits of one's prior activity is due, it is *absolutely impossible* to avoid or evade them. They will surely come home *to the sower* with perfect timing. Be they good or evil, beautiful or ugly, pleasant or painful! And that is not all! As we can grasp from the next principle!

The Fourth Principle: *'This is the Principle of Multiple Returns!'*

Very firmly, it states, "What a man sows, he *must* reap *many times over!*" This means that the right fruits of our *volition seeds* do not only stream back to us at the exact time of due harvest, but they must also unavoidably come back in multiples of what we have sown as seeds by our wishes, thoughts, speech and physical visible actions. This utterly immovable Principle constantly and consistently manifests and asserts itself quite visibly and tangibly down here on Earth. For example, it is very clearly portrayed in our agricultural activities, whereby if, for instance, one sows a seed of corn or mango, the harvest thereafter must bring forth, at the *exact time* of due harvest, multiple seeds of the same kind. And because this outcome very frequently manifests all around us here on Earth and is so commonly perceived in places by everyone, there is absolutely no need for any further explanation on it here!

The only important thing to do here is to relate it to our acts of *free will* and *conscience*. By this, we know that a man who deliberately robs his fellow man, say, of fifty American dollars or one hundred euros, either through cunning or intimidation, must eventually lose *at least* a *hundred times* this amount in consequence when the harvest time is due. The culprit must unavoidably suffer the same loss, the same way, *many times over*, through a similar act of violence or cunning, at the exact time of due harvest. Now, the convinced knowledge of the *absolute unchangeability* of the effects of this great **CUE LAW** is very helpful to a serious *success-seeker*. It actually admonishes and warns one to be very conscious of and to humbly obey the utterly *incorruptible* All-Holy Will of the **ALMIGHTY**, which is constantly expressed, automatically executed by this **CUE LAW**, with absolute accuracy and just severity.

6. The CUE LAW of NATURAL BEAUTY

"Let There Be Light!" Indeed, everything that our great **CREATOR** has brought into existence by this great

Primordial Creative Command is absolutely perfect and defined by supreme beauty! For *Natural Beauty* is an intrinsic quality of the manifestations of His Holy Light throughout this great Creation! Thus it follows that any form of ugliness that exists anywhere on this Earth could only have been brought about by us human beings alone. And that is in direct opposition to the divine Order, which demands that we should always cultivate true *Natural Beauty* in everything that we do here as genuine *part-bearers, pioneers and dispensers* of the Light of our great **MAKER**! If we now really want to make amends, in this regard, in order to restore the true original *Natural Beauty* back into our lives and our environments and thereby ensure our redemption before the **LORD**, we must first and foremost strive to diligently re-learn it again.

We must all make ourselves *genuine* and *keen apprentices* of our **MAKER** in the real science and art of beautiful *Being, Lifestyle* and *Working* down here, in His honour. The right way to that fulfilment is clearly shown to us by His Creation, to which we all belong, thus also by *Nature* which surrounds us everywhere, and which in fact constantly very clearly speaks and visibly and tangibly depicts that *Natural Beauty* in ways which affirm and confirm what our great **LORD** expects of us, His human spiritual creatures. And if we very carefully take a cue from the wonderful work of the Almighty **CREATOR** Himself (i.e., Creation or Nature), this will surely help us to re-awaken the original sense of true *Natural Beauty* given to us by Him. This demands that we carefully observe and learn from *Nature* around us and *correctly* apply for the benefit of all, the following five *principles* operating therein, which jointly express and precisely affirm the **CUE LAW of Natural Beauty**.

The First Principle: **Purity**

Purity! Absolutely *perfect* and *supreme* is the *Natural Beauty,* which characterises all things that were brought into existence by the *Primordial Creative Command* of the Great **CREATOR**. It is therefore very logical to assume that everything employed in the process must thereby also be very *pure* as a *basic condition*. All basic elements that were brought together in the ordained formation of all natural substances which the great builders of this world used, the servants of the Almighty **CREATOR,** must unavoidably have been of the *purest* and, therefore, very best quality, in order to ensure the perfect *Natural Beauty* ordained by the **MOST HIGH**. This logical assertion is very clearly evinced everywhere in nature around us, except where we human beings have tampered with, modified, or distorted the work of nature and thereby devalued its *purity!*

Our earthly environments are currently hardly fit for proper and healthy living for all of us for the simple fact that the *natural purity* of many things has been and continues to be impaired or fouled up. This has indeed very badly destroyed the *Natural Beauty* of the planet given to us as a temporary abode for our growth towards full maturity. So, in order to regain the lost *Natural Beauty* and redeem ourselves, we must take the first step to ensure purity, *natural purity,* living things as nature made and presented them to us in every aspect of our human activity down here, precisely as ordained by our **CREATOR**! For when we have become able to show *real respect* for the *purity* of the work of nature and refrain from distorting it any further, then pure *Natural Beauty*, and, thus, real health will also be reinstated for all of us.

The new culture of *purity*, keeping things *exactly* as the **LORD** wills them to be, which will thereby arise, will then have the *beneficial effects* that these should normally have in our lives. Be it in environmental conditions, nutrition, health care, development and welfare in all aspects of our daily life. And this cannot but make all things more naturally *beautiful* than hitherto! **Purity** is, therefore, of prime *fundamental* significance, wherever we aim seriously to align ourselves with the **CUE LAW Of NATURAL BEAUTY**, that is an imperative *executive* of the *Holy Creative Will* of the **MOST HIGH**. But that is just the beginning, for we must also very keenly always pay due attention to the other equally important *principles*, one of which comes next.

The Second Principle: **Orderliness**

The fulfilment of the *Primordial Creative Command* of the **LORD, "Let There Be Light!"** could not have proceeded in any other fashion except in an absolutely *orderly* one. That is, in view of the *Sublime Perfection,* which is a *Natural Attribute* of the Great **CREATOR** Himself. Hence, its natural effects everywhere on this Earth and in the whole world can never be in any other way than *orderly.* **Orderliness** is therefore a very crucial Principle of the **CUE LAW of Natural Beauty**, which is an *executive* *arm* of the Holy Creative Will of the **ALMIGHTY**. And we must always diligently observe *this* if we really wish to fulfil His Holy Will down here. Very firmly linked to the first principle of *Purity*, it demands that we always strive to ensure a very neat, *methodical,* systematic *arrangement* of things in all aspects of our life and activities, thus in all expressions of our personal *being, lifestyle* and *vocation*, including our thoughts, speech and visible physical deeds.

In order to grasp this requirement aright, let us borrow an example from nature around us by taking a close and careful look at the beautiful creature called the *Butterfly*, its being and its activity. This very fascinating, gentle creature can indeed teach us human beings quite a lot *of things* about this concept of *Orderliness* as an aspect of *Natural Beauty!* Everything about the physical appearance of this very delicate creature quite clearly affirms this principle. Take, for instance, its very proportionate elegant body, as well as the excellently patterned and balanced colourful wings, which altogether portray a very wonderful work of natural art. It very clearly shows the kind of perfect *Orderliness* that accords completely with the **CUE LAW of Natural Beauty**. Look also at the very way this beautiful creature glides about, hovers and perches so lightly on flowers as it fulfils its own unique duty in the activity of nature. It is indeed a glorious celebration of pure, elegant ***Orderliness***.

Really, the way it performs its own role in nature, so effortlessly, is a good reminder to us, *so I believe*, of what is demanded of us humans who are specifically supposed to be the *part-bearers* and *pioneers* of true **Natural Beauty** down here. Again, as it is with the elegant *Butterfly,* so also is it with the many flowers in their colourful varieties. Here we find the natural design with *orderly* arrangements of delicate petals and sepals that are so wonderful and pleasant to behold and even smell. Now, there is absolutely no doubt at all that we humans can take a joyful *cue* from these natural *bearers* and *demonstrators* of the **CUE LAW of Natural Beauty**, which readily abound in our earthly environments, in the forests, natural and man-made gardens, roadsides and other places as well.

The Third Principle: **Balanced Coordination!**

Based upon the solid foundation of *Orderliness,* this principle demands from us the careful bringing together of all parts or things that are *homogeneous or* similar (i.e., of the same nature and thereby *compatible or well-suited* to each other). In the appropriate proportions, the composition of the right forms, shapes, sizes, colours, tones, as well as sounds in order to make them *work together* in such a way as to ensure perfect *equilibrium,* which enables efficiency and effectiveness. Strict fulfilment of this very principle is quite as indispensable as the previous one in every activity that is aimed at the achievement of true natural **BEAUTY** down here. And if we always seriously endeavour to make sure that it is also maintained in all of our human interpersonal relationships and co-operative activities, it naturally unavoidably results in the next value, perfect **Harmony**!

The Fourth Principle: **Harmony!**

Wherever *Purity, Orderliness* and *Balanced Coordination* prevail, in a strictly lawful manner (i.e., in strict accordance with the Holy Will of the **MOST HIGH**), the result is **Harmony,** which is an indispensable factor and standard of true **Natural Beauty**. This is precisely the effect whenever any activity or process is truly in perfect alignment, thus precisely in tune with the *sacred rhythm* of the natural *vibrations* of the Holy Will of the **LORD**, for such an activity or process is then automatically moving or vibrating *in unison, keeping step* with the rate of vibrations of the **CUE LAWS of the LORD,** which naturally express and automatically execute His Holy Will in this Creation. This activity or process then receives such great support from above that an all-around *peaceful* and *happy* experience for all those concerned will naturally follow. And as a crown for all these *principles* stands another great resultant value, which is **Gracefulness!**

The Fifth Principle: **Gracefulness!**

This principle comes forth as the combined effects of the other principles of **Natural Beauty**! And this is due very much to the *pleasant* and *pure joy*-inducing *quality* that always manifests perceptibly in everything that is truly *pure, orderly, balanced, well-coordinated,* and also really *harmonious* in its composition and activity! Thus, to be truly *graceful* is to be really *elegant* and *pleasing* to perceive, both in appearance and in movement. This quality is quite perceptibly consistent in all things that have been brought into life through the activity of the pure and perfect **CUE LAWS of the LORD**, which automatically execute His Holy Creative Will everywhere in this great Creation.

Hence, wherever and whenever any one of these *principles* of *Purity* and *Orderliness*, *Balanced Coordination*, *Harmony* and *Gracefulness* is lacking, really *absent*, there is no natural *Beauty* at all. Consequently, we cannot affirm the fulfilment of the All-Holy Creative Will, **"Let There Be Light!"**, of the Almighty **CREATOR** either. Since this value, Natural Beauty is absolutely inseparable from the All-Holy Light activity! So, let us all henceforth resolutely cultivate pure *Natural Beauty* in all things that we do by strictly observing all of its principles in every aspect of our *Being, our Lifestyle* and in all of our visible earthly *Deeds*. And, thereby, we also joyfully and gratefully honour and glorify our Heavenly **FATHER** Himself. With that said, we conclude our examination of the **CUE LAW of Natural Beauty**. So, let us now move on to explore the great ***Law of Cycle!***

7. The CUE LAW of NATURAL CYCLE

"Let There Be Light!" Here, it is very necessary to recall the fact that the very first **LAW** to manifest in the fulfilment of this Holy *Creative Command* of our great **CREATOR** was the **CUE LAW of Natural Luminosity.** This **CUE LAW,** in its natural cooperation with the **CUE Law of Motion,** which we examined earlier, brought about the projection of living Light into the hitherto dark and empty spaces below and outside the divine realm of eternal light! This lawful event happened in order to promptly ensure the perpetual spreading of the *living Light* from then onward. And the implication for all of us human spirits, who were thereby brought into existence *later on* in the Creative process, was and still is the *need* for constant, consistent and harmonious movements plus the right development towards the perfection of our being, exactly as ordained by our Great **CREATOR**.

To this great need is also attached the fulfilment of the *prime essential purpose* of our conscious existence in this Creation, which naturally lies in the serious fulfilment of the Primordial Creative Command **"Let There Be Light!"**, which indeed bears the glorious prospect of joyful ascent to our original home in Paradise within it, *after* we have really completed our *divinely ordained* spiritual development down here, in this world. This then means the attainment of True Lasting **SUCCESS** in this life. And *that* exactly is where the **CUE LAW of Natural Cycle** comes into the process, as a very significant and most urgent help. In perfect accord with the Holy Will of the **ALMIGHTY**, this **CUE LAW** of our **LORD** very strictly ensures that:

*'Everything that comes from the **starting point**, the Source or Origin of its life, must also unfailingly return to the **starting point** after the completion of its divinely ordained natural development and attainment of its full maturity!'*

This great Creation Law is also known as the **'LAW of ORIGIN'**. For by its *force* and, of course, in collaboration with the other **CUE LAWS of the LORD**, all things must return to their origin, starting point, or even original state of being or position at the very end or completion of their *manifestation!* A very easily perceptible example of the activity of this great **CUE LAW** is that of the transformation of water to vapour, to cloud, and then back to water again, as rain or snow, mist, etc. All being naturally subject to variations in the atmospheric temperature and pressure. Another example is the cycle of the rhythmic flow of blood from the heart of a human being through the various parts of the body and its return to the heart again. There is also the cycle of seasonal changes, which starts with the spring, goes through summer, autumn, winter and back to spring again.

Many other natural examples exist, but the one that is most relevant to us is based on the cycle of our journey through the realms of this Creation under the irresistible force of the **CUE LAW of Natural Cycle**, for it is this **LAW** which collaborates with the other **CUE LAWS** to ensure our ascent back to our place of origin, in Paradise, the spiritual Kingdom of the **ALMIGHTY**, from where we came down to this material world as fresh unconscious *spirit sparks* or else *spiritual seed-grains*. However, this very joyful ending happens only when each one of us has really been, lived, worked, and thus developed himself in the right way here, in this material world, exactly as ordained by our great **MAKER**. That is, through very humble and strict obedience to all of His **CUE LAWS**, including this **CUE LAW of Natural Cycle**.

There is, however, a very special *pre-condition* to be fulfilled by us, which can help us to really benefit from the effects of the **CUE LAW of Natural Cycle**. Every one of us who earnestly seeks to return to his spiritual origin must develop and maintain a very strong, sincere, and passionate longing for the Holy Light **SOURCE** of all life, the **ALMIGHTY**. For this kind of truly serious and sincere longing quite naturally facilitates the supportive activity of this **CUE LAW** in favour of the human being concerned. The living connection brought about by the ardent longing and *true love* for the Almighty **LORD** naturally leads to the upward pulling effect upon the *success-seeker*, which is greatly enhanced by the activity of the **CUE LAW of Natural Cycle.** It is also very important to mention again that all **CUE LAWS** always act together as a single system, although any one of them may have a predominant impact in a particular situation.

For example, the **LAW of Automatic Reciprocity** may *predominate* in the case of a specific redemption of some karmaic debt! But all the **CUE LAWS** will still cooperate to bring about the just result. They are altogether the *sole enablers* and *supporters* of all genuine seekers of *true lasting* **SUCCESS** in this life. We must therefore earnestly strive to grasp them all very thoroughly and strictly obey them always, through conscious and diligent adjustment of ourselves, *inwardly*, to what they demand of us. In this way, they can really help us by their *supportive enabling* activity as we consciously, confidently and very courageously strive along our individual pathways of self-development and joyful ascent upon the **GREAT SUCCESS HIGHWAY!**

FINALLY, it is very worthy of note that the **CUE LAWS of the LORD** are the *natural expressions* and *automatic* *executives* of His Holy Creative Will, expressed as **"Let There Be Light!"** by Which He brought us into existence. The latter is very firmly linked to the **Supreme LAW of the LORD**, the very first of His *Ten Commandments*, which are the *authentic explanations* and *practical interpretations* of His Holy Creative Will. Now this **Supreme Law**, affirmed so by the **Christ**, **JESUS**, is the *highest, holiest* and thus the *greatest* LAW of the **MOST HIGH**, which sternly asserts: **"I... AM THE LORD! THY GOD! THOU *MUST NOT HAVE* ANY OTHER** *GODS...* **BUT ME!"** Thus, we must, above all else, very earnestly strive to *completely surrender* ourselves to the **Almighty LORD** by humbly obeying this **Supreme Law** so that His **CUE LAWS** will then come to our aid *more readily* to faithfully lead and guide us to our glorious *self-fulfilment* upon the **GREAT SUCCESS HIGHWAY**, The **Principled WAY of the MOST HIGH**, **The Purest Surest Path**, where **True SUCCESS** with lasting benefits is happily achieved.

PART 4: The *'Great* SUCCESS HIGHWAY' –
The Principled Way of the MOST HIGH!

Great Success Highway!
Is the 'Principled WAY!' *
The LORD does portray!
To seekers of 'The WAY!'

The **Great SUCCESS HIGHWAY,** the **Purest Surest Path** *of True Lasting* **SUCCESS**, is that of **High Natural Principles** (i.e., **High Moral Rules** and **Values** borne by the pure and perfect **CUE LAWS** of the **LORD** that most accurately express and automatically execute **His Holy Creative Will,** in this great **Creation**!) Hence it is the **'HIGHWAY** of the **MOST HIGH!'** which He most graciously shows to all those human beings who are seriously seeking the **WAY** of *True Lasting* **SUCCESS** in this life. It is *Great* because all activities of the *success-seeker* therein are aimed solely at *honouring* and *glorifying* the **LORD** in steady *Loyalty*, sacred *Faith* and genuine selfless *Love*. And the **SUCCESS** attained thereby is also very real and permanent, for being firmly anchored in and also consistently driven by the **TRUTH**, the power of which alone guarantees continuity of the benefits attained by the fortunate *seeker-finder*!

This Highway, which stretches throughout the entire Creation, is revealed only to those human spirits who have developed and consistently demonstrate real *faith* and *trust* in the **LORD**. Such faithful and trusting ones always *fervently* supplicate for divine help (i.e., divine *instruction, guidance* and *leadership* of the **ALMIGHTY**) in truly *childlike humility* regarding *what* they *must* know and do and *how* to do it aright in order to attain their *life goals* in this world. In response, every earnest suppliant is graciously granted or led to the discovery of the accurate knowledge that will enable him to achieve his goals. It then naturally happens that through his own personal experiences that follow, he will surely gain the firm conviction of the fact that:

In the WORD of the LORD
Surely lies 'The WAY!'
The seeker must find
That will him convey!

He will find that the enabling *High Principles, Moral Rules and Values*, with which the great **LORD** instructs, leads and guides all genuine, faithful seekers to their desired and right goals, are the *elements* of His **CUE LAWS**. And that the true knowledge of these is found *only* in His **Living WORD**. And if, with the aid of one's *Intuitive Faculty*, one tries with *due diligence* always to follow the divine instruction, guidance and leadership given therein, one will surely find the **WAY**. It then becomes much easier to appreciate the great value and high significance of the loving advice which prompts:

Listen to the LORD
Of all the Worlds!
Obey His WORD
And 'The WAY' is yours!

However, **The WAY** does not always remain entirely *trouble-free* for a *success-seeker* down here. This is because of many of our human *faults* and *weaknesses,* which very often arise to *contradict* or *oppose* the **Holy Will** of the **LORD** via our *carelessness* or a lack of adequate *alertness* and constant *ardent prayer* for divine help. Whereby one can be tempted to erroneously begin to think or feel that he can go all the way by his own power *alone.* And it then becomes easier to fall victim to the wrong and fatal schemes of the Darkness, which could lead to complete loss of the **Way!** And this can still happen despite the presence of the great help of the **Lord**, who is always there for all seekers of the **WAY**. For very unfortunately, the Darkness still holds a great deal of influence over this Earth, at the present time, because of our *human unconsciousness* and very careless or wrong use of our *free will power*!

The great influence of the Darkness here on this Earth is, of course, most unfortunately maintained and sustained through its very many *minions, people*, who are always very much active here, everywhere, these days! Their dark and thus hostile activities are aimed solely at distracting and or confusing the true *Light seekers* and diverting them away from the right paths, which are shown by the **LORD** in His **WORD** to all men. Thus, it is now our very urgent duty to be constantly very *alert, prayerful* and *steadfast* in our everyday activities, so that the Power of the LORD can be with, lead, guide and protect us against all machinations of the darkness. We must seriously ensure that we stand firmly upon the **WAY** that is shown to us in His **WORD**, through His given **CUE**

LAWS and **The Ten COMMANDMENTS** contained therein. Otherwise, we risk being led astray, wrongly used, and then maliciously attacked and harmed. It is therefore very urgently necessary indeed that we all earnestly strive to:

Ignore the world!
But stay on 'The WAY!'
For ways of the crowd
Always lead astray!

It also happens that we frequently see around us today many signs or symbols of some human achievements that actually bear a very close external semblance to that of *True* **SUCCESS**. However, on close, deep and careful observation, many of these then prove to be *false* and *transient* because they did not arise from or stand upon the firm basis of the high *spiritual* principles that are contained in the divine **LAWS**, the **CUE LAWS**, of the **ALMIGHTY**. Thus, they can never last or yield lasting benefits because True Lasting **SUCCESS** arises only from serious, strict, and consistent adherence to the **CUE LAWS of the LORD,** which *alone* carry within them true support for the *success-seeker* who fervently prays to the **ALMIGHTY** for it. And who thereby cannot fail to eventually verify for himself, *personally*, the sterling *affirmation*:

SUCCESS that stays
Is found in the rays
The WORD radiates
Unto him that prays!

However, we must always be constantly alert and guard against the tempting acts of the Darkness that could induce carelessness or complacency in us.

We can build up great inner strength against this by continuous spiritual activity, always or regularly absorbing the living and guiding rays of the Word of the **LORD**, and making sure that we resolutely and firmly:

Stand in its Light
And strive aright!
With all our might
Avoid the *night*!

The term ***night*** here means the ***Darkness*** which has been brought about by the fallen archangel *Lucifer.* Who wilfully became Satan, *Antichrist, enemy* of the **ALMIGHTY** and of all those who belong to Him or are seriously seeking and striving towards Him! He *Lucifer-Satan* is the one who, in blatant disregard for the Holy Will of the **MOST HIGH**, wilfully misused the great power given to him to support the right development of men down here. He *malevolently* introduced instead the principle of *loveless temptation,* which then very unfortunately led to the *woeful failure* and the very lamentable *'Fall of man.'* This was the evil deed by which mankind wilfully chose to one-sidedly develop the human intellect of the frontal brain in preference to the superior *spiritual intuitive faculty* which was given to us as a sure link to the **LORD** and **His Kingdom**.

Then earthly humanity went on to develop the intellect so very wrongly and excessively that it resulted in very disastrous intellectual slavery, the adverse fallouts of which we are still grappling with here on Earth to this day. This has unfortunately led to a greater distancing of our humanity from the **CREATOR** for thousands of years now! However, the time has now come for all of us to seriously strive to find our ways back to Him, to work diligently for the very urgently needed salvation and upliftment out of these *dark* realms back to our luminous origin, Paradise. The **WAY** back is very clearly shown to us in the **WORD of the LORD**, first brought to us by the CHRIST **JESUS**, in His message and more recently by **Abdu-ru-shin** in His **'Grail Message – In the Light of TRUTH.'**

Over the past thousands of years, we have been given so much gracious help through the lives and activities of many great servants of the **LORD**, such as Djalfdar, Zoroaster, Laotse, Khrishna, Bhudda and Mohammed, and also through the great prophet Moses. So, there has been, and there is still, an abundance of divine help for all of us residents of this planet Earth, which will most surely enable us to pass and then rise upwards again if we earnestly desire to. And if we very seriously back it up with fervent, childlike and humble supplication for the *divine help* of the great **LORD**, the **WAY** upward will surely be shown to us. As has been said already:

SUCCESS HIGHWAY!
Is the 'Principled WAY!' *
The MOST HIGH Portrays
Unto him, 'that supplicates!'

Finally, we *must never forget* that 'Without the *divine help* of the Almighty **LORD**, it is absolutely impossible for any *success-seeker* to really find his individual path upon the **GREAT SUCCESS HIGHWAY** alone.' Nor can one travel upon it safely and securely without His *high protection*. And it is only via sacred, unshakable *faith* plus very *deep* and *pure trust* in Him, with constant *fervent*, *childlike and humble* supplication, that we can receive His divine help, which will surely lead and guide us safely onward, unto and along this ***Purest Surest Path* of TRUE LASTING SUCCESS**. May we all find It. Amen!

PART 5: THE *SEVEN SUCCESS PRINCIPLES – Building Blocks* of *True Lasting* **SUCCESS!**

NOW, having examined the valuable contents of the preceding parts, we can take a very close and careful look at the **SEVEN SUCCESS PRINCIPLES.** The very highly significant and utterly indispensable *Building Blocks* of True Lasting **SUCCESS,** which every earnest *success-seeker* must acquire, in order to achieve self-realisation. Indeed, these seven *Essential Building Blocks* naturally make up the solid *Mainstay* of the personal effectiveness of a *success-seeker* because the attainment of true lasting **SUCCESS** very strictly depends on how diligently one strives to mould them within oneself. This has to be done in such a way that they always operate harmoniously together, within and through oneself, as an integral whole, for it is *only* through the *conscious* and *balanced* application of these principles that actually define and spell out the word **SUCCESS**, that the desired outcomes can be obtained. Let us now proceed to carefully examine them one by one.

S – *SELF CONSCIOUSNESS*

'Know Thyself!' goes one *time-honoured* counsel. And another, "*Be thou true unto thyself,* and surely as the day follows the night, *thou canst not be false to anyone else!*" (*William Shakespeare*). **Self-Consciousness**, or Self-Knowledge, is an absolutely indispensable personal value that forms the *bedrock* of correct and effective self-development toward perfection. In order to understand this *concept* and its high significance correctly, it is necessary first to ensure that we very clearly grasp its *foundation*, which makes it so crucial. And *that* is the *Divine Creative Volition* by Which the Almighty **CREATOR** brought all of us, human spirits, into existence. This, in an earthly human expression, says:

"Let Us make man in our own image!"... **"According to Our Likeness!"** (*Genesis 1:26 –NKJV*).

Now, if we *seriously* and *humbly* seek to correctly understand the *Divine Aim* contained in these Words, it will surely help us to know about the *specific nature* of the kind of human creatures that the Almighty **CREATOR** actually wished to bring into existence, in this particular case. That understanding will, in turn, help us to know ourselves very well! So, let us start with the first hint that the intended human creatures would be made in His *image,* which as such *must* bear a specific natural *resemblance* to His *'Likeness'* but *not at all* directly to His sublime Self! For **'God is God!'**, He all-exclusively alone! Therefore, we are here dealing with an *absolutely indirect* resemblance and not a direct one at all!

Naturally, His own real *'Likeness'* could be nothing else but *divine*, which as such is absolutely very different from and exceedingly higher than our own human species. Since we are *not divine at all* but only *latter developed human spirits* who were brought into existence in the lowest part of Creation, which is very much below and far away from the divine realm, through the activity of the Holy Creative Will of the **MOST HIGH!** Thus, His true *'Likeness'* must refer strictly only to those *divine beings* who exist and dwell in the divine realm in His own immediate luminous proximity since they are naturally the only ones who can possibly ever bear attributes that most closely reflect His *sublime* ones. That, however, is as far as it is naturally possible for them to do so, by virtue of their being and living in the immediate proximity of the Almighty **CREATOR**.

Logically, then, since we are human spirits of a completely different and *very much lower* species, we can only bear *spiritual attributes* within us that will never come anywhere close at all, not to talk of bearing any *direct resemblance* to the attributes of those divine beings.

In fact, as things stand in this Creation, the prevailing difference in nature normally sets one species apart from and above the other in *status* and *value*. And that is precisely the case between those divine beings, who are very high up in the divine realm, and us human beings down here on Earth, in this very much lower material world.

The divine beings who are the most *original* embodiments of the direct radiations of the great **LORD** are thus the very first *living reflections* and the actual divinely tangible bearers of the true *'Likeness'* of His sublime Attributes. Really, the gap between our own species and that of the divine beings is absolutely and forever unbridgeable! For we are definitely only *spiritual* by nature and not divine at all! Another way to clearly state this fact is to say that we human spirits have *never possessed* and *will never possess* anything of the divine in us unto all eternity! We only came into existence first as unconscious spirit germs or sparks in the lowest part of Spiritual Creation. Those who, in the *latter* part of spiritual evolution, became *developed human spirits*, not at all *directly created beings*. Those whose development actually happened in this material world, *outside* the spiritual realm, which is our true origin, very, very far away from the divine realm. We therefore belong to a species of beings that can bear only *spiritual attributes* within us, by virtue of our nature, which is basically spiritual only.

The divine is purely and strictly forever divine, while the spiritual is similarly forever spiritual. *This* is the fact that any one of us who really desires an exact *Self-Knowledge* for the purpose of gaining *true lasting* **SUCCESS** in this life must always very clearly and firmly bear in mind. That we are naturally only *latter developed* human spirits who took on form as such through the Creative Will of the Almighty **CREATOR**. Thus, we only bear within us those *spiritual attributes* which can *very remotely* spiritually reflect the divine Attributes of our great **LORD**. However, this very same condition is the sure natural basis and support for any one of us who earnestly strives for true *childlikeness* to be able to attain it at the very definite point of his full maturity and perfection as a true, *fully self-conscious* human being, as willed by the **LORD!**

The above statements are very important in helping us to avoid any wrong assumptions or, worse still, any presumption about our actual *status, value* and *exact position* in this Creation because of the indisputable fact that our own species is indeed the *lowest* of all that is spiritual, which are made in *human form* by the Creative Will of our **MAKER**.

This means that we human spirits of this Earth, or *earthmen*, are *not at all* the *prime spiritual images* of our great **CREATOR** either! A very irrefutable fact that stands *directly opposed* to the wrong opinion of so many of us today. For there are some among us who *erroneously* believe that they are also *divine!* Whereas by the authentic knowledge that one can grasp through the great *Spiritual Work*, **'In The Light Of Truth – The Grail Message'** by **Abd-ru-shin**, the true *spiritual images* of our great **LORD** are indeed the *prime spiritual beings*, the *very first spiritual beings* to come alive in the foremost and highest part of this great Creation, following the divine utterance of the *Primordial Creative Command* **"Let There Be Light!"**.

But we, the *latter developed human beings* of this world, who had to first grow from spirit sparks or spirit germs, just like some earthly *fruit trees* germinate from seed grains, are actually the very last *spiritual copies* of those *prime spiritual beings* who came first into existence a very long time ago before we did. However, the fact that we belong to the very last ramifications of spiritual images of our great **MAKER** does not devalue us at all, before Him and in this Creation. Indeed, we should be very proud, grateful and really happy on that account because not only are we His human spiritual creatures and the *indirect images* as explained above, but we are also spiritual *part-bearers* and *dispensers* of His Light. Exactly as the Christ **JESUS** stated about us while He was down here, on His great Mission of Salvation: *"You are the Light of this world!"* And that means each one of us bears a *spiritual spark* of the *Light Power* of our **MAKER** within him. By this Light Power of the Almighty **LORD**, each one of us is supposed to be, live and work diligently aright, always spreading His Light all around, according to His Holy Will.

That is, if one seriously wishes to assure his own true lasting SUCCESS here on this Earth, and generally in this great Creation. In addition, we do have another great cause for joy, in the fact that we also bear within us a very great gift, *a truly unique potentiality*, by the special grace of our **MAKER**, to become His *adopted children* forever! Wow!… Just think of *that* for a minute! Becoming and then being a *human spiritual child* of the great LORD, the Absolute, Almighty RULER of all realms of Existence, unto all eternity! And say, now, fellow *success-seeker*, if that is not so very wonderful enough as to make each one of us to really jump for great joy, coupled with a very firm and strong resolve to always earnestly strive to achieve that most glorious status at all reasonable costs!

I am very sure that you will agree with me that this is very much so! And it is just for that very reason that we *must* now seriously strive to mould those essential *Building Blocks of true* **SUCCESS** within us, starting with this first block **S**, for **Self-Consciousness.**

Self-consciousness is indeed naturally a *two-part value,* just like a peanut is made of two halves. The first part reveals the *natural essence* of our being, which is *spiritual,* and which thereby affirms our *Essential Identity* as *Spiritual!* As has been said earlier, *we* start as unconscious *spirit* *sparks* with the capacity to develop and acquire the *human form* as we gradually gain *self-consciousness* while maturing and becoming more powerful. This is how we progressively become real human beings who may bear within us true and pure *childlike attributes* that really qualify us to be regarded from on high as authentic *developed human spiritual images* of our Almighty **MAKER**.

Those who have ultimately attained the status of *true children* of the **LORD**, in very strict accordance with His Holy Will. In fact, we have all been given the *pure potentialities* for achieving *this* by our **LORD** right from the very start of our existence!

These naturally include the seeds of very pure attributes, with corresponding attitudes and aptitudes which, when fully developed into full executive powers, can be actively applied to our being, living and working aright in fulfilling the Holy Will of our **MAKER**.

It is also very important to state here that we all have these gifts in common, given to all of us equally from the very start as potentialities. This means that any differences in our personalities, lifestyles and modes of working have only arisen, over time, from the diverse ways in which we have individually chosen to develop and apply those talents in our lives. On the part of our **MAKER,** however, there has never been any favouritism or partiality of any kind at all. Nor will there ever be because He is absolutely *consistently* perfect and impartial!

Now, following our grasp of the fact that our ***Essential Identity***, that is the ***'what'*** of us, is spiritual, we can now proceed to view its *natural counterpart*, thus the ***'who'*** of our true being, which is very firmly linked to it. This is the **Functional Identity** that arises from how man has chosen to develop all of his natural gifts, personal qualities or character traits plus his abilities, in the course of time, into a *unique* combination that surely has a very decisive and incisive bearing on his *true personal vocation* and how he performs it down here. And guess where this **Functional Identity**, the **'who'** of a human being, is based! It is very securely based in and thereby clearly portrayed by the person's **name**! Yes, it is precisely the **name** of a person that exactly says **who** he really is, which also indicates quite clearly and correctly what his *true personal vocation* down here is.

A person's real **name** is the *word form* of the bundle, the totality of his natural powers and qualities which he has come to actively express here on Earth. Thus it follows that any *success-seeker* who truly wishes to know his own innate talents and powers in order to be able to properly awaken and develop them, and to thereby really *actualise* and perfect the unique *meaning* of his own being, which will also facilitate the effective fulfilment of his *prime essential purpose* of life, here on Earth, and in the entire CREATION, must *first* seriously seek to clearly and correctly know the exact *meaning* and the real *significance* of his own **name**. Indeed, it is a very well-known fact, in some earthly cultures, that a human being is invariably very strongly influenced, *in everything,* by his *real* **name**. With this crucial knowledge of man's **Functional Identity**, which is firmly and securely linked with his inner being, thus with his **Essential Identity**, the requisite **Self-consciousness** is complete.

However, the *upbuilding* process of this great value does take some time, just like the lifelong process of true **SUCCESS** that it collaborates to define. It comes forth gradually through earnest, constant and consistent growth, led and guided by the Holy Will of the **ALMIGHTY**. It is similar to that of a mango tree, which, after attaining fruit-bearing age, still continues to mature and bring forth more and better fruits each season. Thus, with the gaining of this special value, *Self-consciousness* (which grows clearer and deeper with time), one is also enabled to recognise more clearly, correctly and deeper still his life's *vocation,* which constantly fires in one, an ardent urge for his correct, *useful* and joyful *activity* down here.

This process is always very much *enhanced* and *quickened* by one's fervent, childlike, and humble supplication to the **MOST HIGH** for His divine help, guidance and enabling leadership at all times. For *"Ask, and you shall receive!" "Seek, and you shall find!" "Knock, and it shall be opened unto you!"* – **The Christ, JESUS**. The sure result of that act of humble supplication is the gaining of very *definite enlightenment* and *clarity,* which motivates the seeker to diligently pursue the moulding also of the next profitable *Building Block,* **U,** which stands for *Usefulness.*

U – USEFULNESS!

Usefulness is the *conscious* and *diligent* fulfilment of a specific and *beneficial* purpose in life by effectively performing one's definite roles, responsibilities and duties in line with one's *exact meaning* and *prime essential purpose* of life and in *strict accordance* with the Holy Will of the Almighty **LORD**. Thus, as far as we are concerned, this has a very close and unbreakable connection with the first *Building Block* of true **SUCCESS,** which we have just examined (i.e., ***Self-Consciousness***). What is now very important to affirm here is the fact that a person's *vocation, personal calling*, or *earthly activity* can be said to be *useful* only if it is firmly aligned with, and most diligently serves, the Holy Will of the **ALMIGHTY**, His *Primordial Creative Command*, which is expressed as *"Let There Be Light!"*.

The human being is created by and also partly bears a *spiritual element* of this Holy Command within himself as an eternal *Operational and Appraisal Standard* for his own being, lifestyle and work down here. And for the necessary ethical combating, *without violence* or devastation, for what is really good and just, whenever it is really necessary, and in strict accordance with the Holy Will of the **LORD**. Please take very careful note here that being a *part-bearer* of a *spiritual element* of the Holy Creative Will of the Almighty **LORD** simply means that a spiritual particle of a ray of this Creative Will was originally embedded in the spirit of man right from the start of its life, so that it can serve as an eternal inner prompt for the human being concerned to always be, live and work aright by It and in It forever!

That is if man really wishes to fulfil the Holy Will in order to attain *true* **SUCCESS** with *lasting benefits* in his life. Every human being also possesses the *free will* to choose and act as he wishes and inescapably to bear full responsibility for the consequences. Thus, if a person chooses to pursue an occupational path that is against his nature and natural talents given to him for his life down here by the Almighty **LORD**, he is only serving his own intellectual or worldly agenda and may then not expect to achieve *true lasting* **SUCCESS** thereby. This lies strictly *only* in the fulfilment of the Holy Will of the **CREATOR**. All that a person like that may eventually get in return will be temporary glory, at best in the form of *transient earthly accomplishment*. And in the worst case, life without any joy at all!

To really recognise one's ***Useful Purpose*** of existence here, in addition to one's ***Self-Consciousness***, in the light of the Creative Will of the Almighty **LORD**, is fundamental to the achievement of real permanent ***Prosperity***. Therefore, we must not take this very crucial *building block* lightly at all but strive earnestly to grasp it correctly. The correct knowledge of one's ***Useful Purpose*** in life is thus very important in that it helps one to pursue correct *vocational development* and the right activities here on Earth. Each one of us can then cooperate harmoniously with our own vocational kind in order to produce really *valuable* and *useful* things for the benefit of fellow human beings, who must then also reciprocate accordingly.

It is through this kind of useful *homogeneous cooperation* that we are enabled to really honour and glorify the great **LORD**, because such harmonious and beneficial work quite naturally conforms with His Holy Creative Will. The great importance of supplicating to the **LORD** for His divine help in this regard also cannot be over-emphasised, for it is only the Almighty **CREATOR** Who really knows the exact *purpose* for which He has made man and given him all those natural talents which are required for fulfilling it.

It is thus very sensible and wise that we should *ask Him first* for His divine guidance before going on to seriously invest our energies, talents and time in any kind of work! *"Ask and you shall receive!"* – the **Christ**. But this we seldom do because we generally tend to feel that we know better or are wise enough to decide for ourselves. Whereas, if we have formed the good habit of always *Asking, Seeking and Knocking* first, in fervent, childlike and humble supplication for the divine guidance and leadership of our **LORD**, in all circumstances, before we begin any activity, millions of us who have done and are still doing all kinds of *wrong* and joyless jobs today, here on this Earth, would surely be pursuing other totally self-fulfilling, useful and very happy activities instead. There would then have been so much more useful and happier activities that would really ensure far greater peace and joy, ennoblement, and lasting prosperity plus blissful upliftment for us all today. Rather than the so chaotic, miserable conditions that we now have in so many places down here on Earth at the present time. All due to our rather careless, superficial attitude regarding this important matter to date. I am quite sure, fellow *success-seeker,* that you know very well what I am saying here.

One only needs to look attentively around our earthly environments today, without too much effort or racking one's brain intensely, to confirm the truth of this very adverse result of our general attitude to this very serious matter. However, through our fervent, childlike, and humble supplication to the All-Wise **CREATOR** for His perfect guidance, the correct ways will certainly be shown to every one of us, very simply and timely, too. Most especially true if we hold *pure, unshakable faith* and *confidence* in Him, plus the necessary *alertness* and *openness* of mind. And it is then with joyful *conviction* that the *divinely guided* one will consciously and *confidently* pursue his own clearly recognised *vocation*, which perfectly corresponds to his natural gifts, talents and virtues, thereby performing his correct and useful *Roles, Responsibilities and Duties*, as expressions of his own personal meaning, in the fulfilment of his prime essential purpose of existence. So, what is crucial and most conditional for self-fulfilment in this matter is the humble seeking for the divine guidance of the **ALMIGHTY** and then *committing* oneself to It wholeheartedly!

C – COMMITMENT

A serious *success-seeker* who has acquired accurate **Self-Consciousness** and the exact knowledge *of his Useful Purpose in life,* has thereby obtained two highly essential *Building Blocks* of true lasting **SUCCESS.** But it is the serious and very tenacious inner *Commitment* to the fulfilment of his *life Purpose* which actually helps him to establish that *steady Focus* which is needed for achieving the sought-after goals of life. And what precisely does one need to ensure this *Commitment?* It is simply ***True Selfless Love!*** The greatest of all values and forces alive, which strongly links its true bearer to the **Source** of all Life, the eternal inexhaustible **Fountain** of all life energies! This Great Value, ***True Love***, can be expressed as *'Absolutely pure, perfect and consistent, wholehearted, wholeminded, all-embracing and selfless Goodwill!'*

It is this genuine *good-willing Power*, the greatest *divine* gift that a man can ever bear within, *True Love*, which enables him to develop that serious, steady and unswerving devotion that unfailingly gets the desired results. Driven by this power, the *success-seeker* is able to seriously pursue the specific activity that is dictated by his clearly recognised purpose. This, of course, happens naturally as the one concerned resolutely exerts his true *love-driven* volition to do something that will be of real benefit to the wider environment, human and material, in accordance with the Holy Creative Will of the **MOST HIGH**. The ardent desire to deliver real values to others then moves him inwardly, by the special high guidance, towards the exact Roles, Responsibilities and Duties which are in perfect resonance with his natural talents and virtues.

It is only always this very kind of volition that attracts the necessary help to a genuine *success-seeker*, which enables him to really prosper in this life. The supportive events required by him will so manifest around him in such a favourable manner that he becomes so clear within himself always about what he must do. The powerful guidance from on high never allows him to err or fail at all. Here he is naturally *'In the Stream!' and* can consciously feel the vibrant energy of life streaming through him, awakening deep emotions of pure joy of being helped by the Almighty **LORD** within him. And this is what strongly assures the seeker that he is definitely in the right activity and place.

All due to his serious and strong sense of *Commitment*, which is driven by the power of *True Selfless Love*. That of a genuine desire *to* do something of value that will benefit and uplift one's general environment. Now, the fact that the *success-seeker* knows that he has the latent abilities required for the realisation of his life Goals will give him the joyful motivation and triumphant courage to pursue the development of those requisite *Vocational Competences* (i.e., attitudes, knowledge and skills which define and enable excellent performance and fulfilment of his roles, responsibilities and duties). These, in turn, ensure real *permanent Prosperity*. Let us now move on to examine the fourth relevant *Building Block*, **C**, *Competence!*

C – COMPETENCE!

COMPETENCE! A highly significant and absolutely indispensable *Building Block* of true lasting **SUCCESS!** It is the *ability to do* something *consistently* well, up to the required standards of *Excellence!* The truly **committed** or devoted *success-seeker* is always driven by such a compelling inner urge for valuable achievement that he always feels ready and very willing to *learn* and really *know* and *do* whatever *good things* it takes to prosper in his life *Vocation*. Thereby, he works diligently to acquire those *vocational competencies* required for an excellent delivery of the *specified quality* of work or else service in every aspect of his field of practice! He will, therefore, strive to develop his innate talents (i.e., *latent Attributes, Attitudes* and *Aptitudes*) to full executive powers, which he needs to add real values to a good cause in which he is involved and through which he may then naturally reap real values back.

He then stands qualified and ready to fill the post that he is meant to hold here on Earth, in *perfect attunement* with his prime essential purpose of life, as a human spiritual *part-bearer, pioneer* and dispenser of the Holy Creative Will of the Almighty **LORD**, exactly according to his own nature. So, a *success-seeker* who bears the essential *Building Blocks* of *Self-consciousness, Usefulness* and *Commitment* still needs to strive to really become *competent* in his *vocation,* in order to *actualise* the *unique meaning* of his being or personality and thereby fulfil his prime essential *purpose* of conscious existence. He must be constantly *what* and *who* he is meant to be, himself, with an exact *lifestyle* that really corresponds to his being while working effectively in his vocational field. Also, he must become competent in the art of fighting aright, ethically, *without violence*, for what is good and just, in his own natural circle of influence, strictly in accordance with the Holy Will and **CUE LAWS** of the Almighty **LORD**.

This means that a competent person is, in reality, the one who is *being* exactly as the **LORD** wills him to be, a true human being living a corresponding *lifestyle* and, as such, performing all of his specific *Roles, Responsibilities and Duties* aright, in such a way that they may then count as pure *reverential Worship* of the Almighty **LORD**. NOW, it is very important to state here that there is no *real-life* vocation that cannot be turned into genuine worship of the **LORD** in this world, if one really wishes to do so. All it takes is to ensure that one chooses the *right activity* and adjusts it completely to His Holy Will. And how exactly, *you may ask*, can one find his own sure way thereto? It is, **again**, *strictly* through fervent, childlike, and humble supplication for the *divine Help* of the All-Wise **CREATOR**, our **LORD**! For *"Ask, and you shall receive!"*, *"Seek, and you shall find!"* *"Knock and it shall be opened unto you!"*. Absolutely unfailingly!

In addition, there is ample supportive guidance and leadership given to us in the Living **WORD** of the **LORD,** which we can very easily access through His *divine Messages* sent down to us over the ages! Therein, we will surely find the pointers to the authentic knowledge that we require for this. Whether it is about this great Creation to which we all belong, the Holy Will of our **LORD** and His perfect **CUE LAWS** that operate therein, or most especially the **Ten Commandments of GOD** that very clearly explain and also interpret His Holy Will in practical terms for all of us to follow. Through the constant exercise of diligently absorbing the **WORD of the LORD**, backed with regular humble prayers for His divine support, the correct relevant illumination or inspiration and direct guidance will surely be obtained.

So very clearly and correctly will the supplicant eventually grasp the knowledge of his correct earthly vocation that he becomes able to consciously, confidently, awaken from within himself *that great power* which was given to him personally by the **ALMIGHTY**, for his joyous, productive, and useful activity down here. Lively **Enthusiasm!** Another great *Building Block,* which we meet next!

E – ENTHUSIASM!

NOW, when a serious *success-seeker* consciously, deliberately awakens that inner (**En**) *spiritual power* of the Almighty **DEITY** (***Theus***), which is constantly *streaming* through him for a *joyful* and *useful* activity (***Ism***), in his fulfilment of a specified valuable goal or purpose, that is **Enthusiasm** in the truest sense of the concept! Naturally, all activities of man are driven from within him by the use of this inner spiritual power, which, as such, also enables one to operate consciously and deliberately in a focused manner when in pursuit of any special or worthy objectives. Hence, in order to awaken this power, which is different from the energy of the physical body, all one needs to do is simply to deliberately switch it on, by one's spiritual volition, *free will,* plus intuition in collaboration with one's conscience (faculty of morality), and thereby link up with the intellect or the power of thought.

This act is greatly enhanced by being always *conscious* that one carries this great *executive power* from the Almighty **LORD** within oneself, also that it is backed and driven by His Omnipotence if one humbly opens oneself to it! The very thought that one has the help of the Great Power of the **MOST HIGH** behind one's own volition helps very much in being able to generate the *inner intuitive picture* of the object of one's desire. It also helps one to awaken the *calm confidence* and *triumphant courage* which are required for an accomplishment. Therefore, it is very important that we never forget to ensure that we always have the Will Power of the **LORD** behind our own, whenever we have to perform any special, serious or truly worthy tasks that require one's real *enthusiasm.*

However, we must be fully aware of the great responsibility that we bear in this process and make sure that we do not use the power called forth thereby for any base or wrong or evil purposes. All intuitions, thoughts, spoken words and visible physical deeds must be pure and aimed at positive, progressive, and uplifting outcomes for all concerned. The opposite will surely bring back painful results to the one concerned.

For *"Whatsoever a man sows, that exactly must he reap many times over!"* and *"As a man sows must he reap!"* Exactly as the Christ, **JESUS**, very sternly warned us all!

Thus, truly beneficial *Enthusiasm* requires *the support* of the Omnipotence of our **LORD** coupled with our own ***Self-control***, which is the next object of our examination.

S – SELF-CONTROL!

Self-control, self-discipline! A very powerful and reliable *building block* of true lasting **Success** in this life! The *golden* distinctive mark of every *mature Personality* who has acquired *Total Self-mastery!* The latter naturally develops from the first Building Block of true lasting **SUCCESS** (i.e., **Self-consciousness**). Self-control is the innate ability of the human being by which he consciously, resolutely and forcefully directs his free will or volition, his intuition and conscience, emotions and feelings, as well as his thoughts, his speech and physically visible deeds to a definite point of action, in a very determined and focused manner which ensures the desired results.

Surely, everyone who is seriously seeking true and lasting **SUCCESS** in this life *must* be very aware that the *best* and *surest* way to achieve it lies *only* in one's ability and the willingness to strictly, consistently and *very humbly* obey the very pure and perfect **CUE LAWS** which naturally express and automatically execute the All-Holy Will of the great **LORD,** in this Creation.

The compelling necessity for this consistent obedience is dictated by the fact that the seeker's journey along the **GREAT SUCCESS HIGHWAY** in this world is unavoidably full of many challenges that he can never overcome by himself *alone*. There are many obstacles that will surely emerge from time to time on the *Way* that will put his strength of character and resolve to serious test. Also, there may sometimes be painful frustrations and disappointments, which can bring irritation, suffering, or discouragement, just as there is also an unlimited Grace of Divine Help, Support and Protection from on High at the same time! It is thus the sacred duty of the *success-seeker* to remain vigilant and to be very firmly in control of his own senses and abilities.

One must definitely always be very alert, both *spiritually* and *materially*, and thereby be able to perceive the true nature or essence of any approaching events or circumstances correctly, which may carry any danger or temptations that can quite easily make him lose self-control, fail and fall! That is, to fall into sin against the **CUE LAWS** of the **LORD** by letting himself go and thereby incurring guilt or bad karma. We must always recall the golden *Counsel* of Christ **JESUS,** which says, *"Watch and pray... So that you may not fall in temptation!"* This is exactly why we must develop *Self-control* power, through first acquiring the very crucial *self-mastery*, coupled with constant rightful use of our *free will power!*

For this purpose, we must always remember to ardently ask for strength and divine guidance from the All-Wise, Almighty **LORD**, who is very capable of giving us the strength to courageously face all challenges and the attacks of Lucifer's minions victoriously. This is also how we are able to develop that toughness of will that forcefully rejects all that is wrong. Wrong in the context of evil enticements from the realms of *Darkness and Hell,* which can make a person violate the **CUE LAWS** of the **ALMIGHTY**. Indeed, it is quite true that the constant exercise of *Self-control* naturally helps one to progressively develop another great personal quality, which is very beneficial. And that is **Patience**! This ability to stay very calm and stable, without anger or agitation, in the face of any challenging or unpleasant event which can cause one to lose one's temper and then fall, requires a great deal of *Self-control.*

Only a *self-controlled* person has the energy and time to exercise the great power of *Patience.* It is only he who has the capacity to effectively utilise the *space* and *time* at his disposal for the very necessary deep *inner reflection* that is required for gaining a clear understanding of any challenging circumstance that he is confronted with at any given time. He is the one who can fully exercise *due introspection* and *restraint* within the *time* and *space* existing between an *external action* and his own necessary *response* to it! This quite naturally helps one to carefully decide and then act aright firmly for positive outcomes or solutions. It is thus obvious that *Self-control* can really help one to exercise the necessary *patience* that is needed for correct understanding, consideration, and right judgement as well as taking the right course of action, which is required for getting the desired good results.

It can be said, therefore, that a *self-controlled* person has the ability to direct his own *free will*, intuition, conscience, wishes, temperaments, thoughts, speech and physically visible deeds *consciously* toward the desired goals. There will then be neither superficiality nor carelessness, nor any impulsive behaviours at all! What is also certain is that a *self-controlled* person never attends to his own Roles, Responsibilities and Duties casually or wantonly. He can also really be *flexible* whenever it is necessary by listening carefully to other points of view, thereby examining all possible options before taking a final and wise decision. It is, therefore, quite easy for the *Self-controlled* success-*seeker* to develop and manifest the qualities of *Humble Flexibility* instead of conceited *Rigidity that* very often leads to utter failure, conflicts and avoidable unhappiness.

In fact, *Self-control* enables one to always remain focused and to firmly keep one's goals in mind and thereby be able to give due priority to the most urgent and important matter first. Finally, it directly facilitates the unfolding of another great ability which caps the set of the wonderful *Building Blocks* of *true lasting* **SUCCESS**... *Steadfastness*! Let us now go for it!

S – STEADFASTNESS

In the examination of the preceding *building block*, **Self-Control**, we have found that the self-controlled *success-seeker* bears the sterling quality of **Patience** within, which enables him to exercise deep **Consideration**, **Humility** *and* **Flexibility**. Occasionally, however, both personal and external factors could still arise in such a way that one may lose his self-control, even for a brief moment, despite one's great determination. Yes, it may just so happen that the situation or an event suddenly becomes *uncontrollable* or *overwhelming*! In such circumstances, which are described as being naturally beyond one's control, when, for instance, some terrible personal or other catastrophes, natural or man-made, may happen. There could also be some life-threatening happenings like sudden attacks, illnesses, accidents or even bereavements, etc.

And guess *what*! Life itself sometimes brings up some of its own powerful challenges, *especially purposefully*, which are aimed at compelling the seeker to awaken his own divinely bestowed powers for the fight when only a tough *fight-and-no-flight* attitude is advantageous! Face to face with these kinds of circumstances, even an *enthusiastic*, *self-controlled* and earnest *success-seeker* may sometimes find himself completely at a loss regarding what to do next! That is exactly when and why one must awaken a much higher power from within oneself that is absolutely capable of keeping him on course and to keep holding on, sternly striving onward until *Total Victory* is won. And that *rock-steady, unconquerable capacity* is called **Steadfastness!**

A very tough, very resilient, indomitable mental attitude that absolutely refuses to give up trying or fighting on in the face of whatever adversity. A kind of *fight-to-the-finish* mindset! And dear *fellow seeker*, can you guess what is the actual power that lies within and forcefully drives this great capability? It is **Faith**, *Pure Active* **Faith**! Which naturally and quite instantly springs forth from the firm, unshakable *Conviction*, absolute *Certainty*, of the great divine *Help* of the **MOST HIGH**, which is always available for all truly faithful seekers! Those human beings who very deeply and unshakably trust in Him! This firm trust has, of course, been developed through several real-life experiences of the very special grace of the pure **LOVE** of the great **CREATOR** over time.

It naturally comes with the sacred and intimate assurance of the *success-seeker* that the Almighty **LORD**, in His great *Loving-Kindness*, never forsakes anyone who truly has and exercises genuine and unshakable *Trust* in Him. At any time of very urgent or most desperate need. **Steadfastness!** It consistently helps one to remain very focused, psychologically and emotionally balanced and stable in such a way that one is enabled to *faithfully*, that is, consciously, confidently and courageously maximise the benefits of his own serious efforts. One more important factor is as follows: In addition to being driven by the power of *pure active* **Faith**, the present quality of **Steadfastness** is also greatly enhanced by the *complete certainty* of the absolute *necessity* and *worthiness* of a given or chosen good and beneficial cause. This also explains why the truly earnest *success-seeker* never thinks of giving up his serious striving, and thereby, true **SUCCESS** with lasting benefits is most certainly assured for him.

He just continues vigorously and steadily *striking the hammer* until the hard *kernel of good fortune* eventually splits open, thereby yielding its valued contents to him! And in the realisation that this could not have come about at all *without* the Help of the **LORD**, which he had fervently sought, in very humble childlike supplication to Him, very jubilant gratitude then springs forth spontaneously from his heart. And truly, there is absolutely no difficulty, no opposition, barrier or attacks of the minions of *Lucifer, the Anti-Christ*, who abound everywhere upon this Earth today, that can ever overcome any truly *faithful* and *steadfast* one. For the great **LOVE** of the Almighty **LORD** always watches over, protects, defends and preserves such an earnest human spirit who really humbly and faithfully trusts in Him. He, our great **LORD**, always mercifully shows all such people the *right way out* of all difficult situations, through the leadership and guidance of His Divine Wisdom, onward to *Victory*, total permanent Victory! And where exactly does an earnest *success-seeker* find the *Spiritual Food and Drink* that he requires for building up within himself that great victorious power, *pure* active ***Faith***, which enables and drives his **Steadfastness?**

It is precisely in the Living **WORD** of the **LORD**. In fact, all of the Building Blocks of true lasting **SUCCESS** we have examined so far can be built up within oneself *only via* the correct absorption of the contents or the essence of the Living **WORD** of the **LORD**. Starting with the fundamental **S**elf-Consciousness, **U**sefulness, **C**ommitment and **C**ompetence, plus **E**nthusiasm, **S**elf-Control and finally, **S**teadfastness! Just by taking the ***WORD*** of the **LORD** resolutely as the *firm* and *all-exclusive* basis of one's earnest striving for the development of these Values as personal qualities and *powers*, and also by allowing oneself to be strictly led and guided by the perfect **CUE LAWS** of the **LORD** and His **Ten Commandments** contained therein, one can thereby align himself with the living and supporting rays of the Holy Creative WILL of the **MOST HIGH**. Indeed, very great is the motivation that lies in the firm *conviction* that one is, by the special grace of the **ALMIGHTY**, a human spiritual *part-bearer* and *pioneer* of His Light, which thus embraces His Love, Justice and Purity, Peace, Joy and Beauty with Harmony down here on Earth.

For if with that consciousness one always makes genuine efforts at manifesting these Attributes of the **LORD** as he should, in all aspects of his being, lifestyle and vocational activity, he will surely gradually grow more luminous, loving, peaceful, joyful, beautiful and thereby *powerful*! He then becomes more competent to spread all these attributes, gifts of the **LORD**, all around himself spiritually in a more effective and uplifting manner. He is thus enabled to inwardly experience, sense deeply within himself the essence of the *living word* of the Christ, **JESUS**: "You are *the Light* of this World!". At this stage, the *success-seeker* becomes more able to intuitively grasp things within and around himself much more clearly and correctly than before. And so, with the acquisition of this great capacity for clearer, deeper and balanced perception, one can earnestly pursue his life goals more **steadfastly**, with the firm assurance of attaining them. Thereby, one can very *gradually* build up for himself the great and wonderful quality of *Total Personal Excellence*, **TOPEX**. The exploration of which comes next.

PART 6: Total Personal EXCELLENCE – The *Real Essence* of **True Lasting SUCCESS!**

It may happen that a *success-seeker* gets curious about how it is possible that the attainment of those named *Essential Building Blocks* of true lasting **SUCCESS**, like **S**elf-consciousness and **U**sefulness, **C**ommitment, **C**ompetence, **E**nthusiasm, **S**elf-control and **S**teadfastness, can actually enable an earnestly *seeking person* to achieve the *extraordinary* quality that is called *Total Personal Excellence*, briefly **TOPEX**. The simple answer is that this great value, **TOPEX**, is the *natural outcome*, an unavoidable effect of all the *earnest efforts* which a serious *success-seeker* has been very diligently putting into the process of moulding those *Building Blocks* within himself so that they then consequently become an integral part of him as personal qualities and *executive powers*!

This happens, of course, because the diligent *success-seeker* has meticulously grasped these powerful *principles* in such a manner that they are linked together as real *building* blocks, which consequently and most certainly unite to elevate him thus. Indeed, it is precisely via this process that the relevant capabilities are then developed, which quite naturally reveal and affirm the *success-seeker's* exceptional quality of *Total Personal Excellence.* Naturally, it simply shines through quite visibly in all aspects of the *Being*, corresponding *Lifestyle*, as well as *Vocational Activity* of the person concerned. And it comes across sharply also when, sometimes, the *serious Combat* for what is *good* and *just, in exact accordance with the Holy Will of the Almighty* **LORD**, becomes necessary.

At those times when an *earnest seeker* must do battle, although *without violence or any devastation*, against all those challenges or attacks that may appear on his way. You know, those times when the genuine seeker of true **SUCCESS** unexpectedly or even unavoidably finds himself confronted with hostile opposition of some adversaries while he is resolutely striving onward, performing his due Roles, Responsibilities and Duties. Here, some of the true marks of *Excellence* that are called forth are the same *sterling* qualities that directly assure true lasting **SUCCESS:** *Self-consciousness, Self-control, Enthusiasm, as well as Steadfastness.* Very urgently needed then, above all, is the great power of *Faith, Holy Unshakable Faith*, plus its constant, consistent, very close allies (i.e., *Fearlessness* and *Triumphant Boldness*).

These circumstances invariably call for a very firm, determined inner attitude that very strongly and courageously rejects all forms of *injustice* or *unfair treatment* from others while at the same time avoiding *deliberately or wantonly* acting unjustly, causing any harm to them, in the process. The *success-seeker* who has truly reached this stage in his striving is thus working according to the Holy Will of the **ALMIGHTY**, WHO has ordained that all of us, His *human spiritual creatures*, must strive diligently for true *Perfection* in all aspects of our lives. And to strive for whatever goals we desire without *deliberately* harming or knowingly causing any suffering, pain and sorrow at all to our fellow men thereby. For that kind of *very tough restraint alone is the real proof of true Perfection before Him.*

"Become ye therefore perfect as your Father Who Art in Heaven is Perfect!" says the CHRIST, **JESUS**, who, in another instance, also advised all of us: *"Whatsoever your hands findeth to do, do it well."* And coming from the **CHRIST**, *'Doing it well'*, in this case can be very safely assumed to mean that one must strive for a very high, indeed *the very best standard* of performance and attainment ever possible. But absolutely doing so in a very *ethical* and *just* manner always! Even in all acts of *self-defence,* perfect Justice remains absolutely inseparable from the true Love of our **LORD** and must therefore reign supreme (i.e., must be maintained!), which again accords with another golden advice of the Christ; *"Love thy neighbour as thyself!"*

OR What do you think? I am sure He means we should all strive for the utmost level of *Excellence* in all things, in whatever good things we choose or have to do, without hurting our fellow men deliberately thereby. Therefore, **TOPEX** is so very essential that one must really strive to grasp its concept thoroughly. But first, one has to correctly understand the great *concept* of true **EXCELLENCE** as a matter of necessity.

EXCELLENCE is the *distinctive quality* of being *exceptionally* good. Both in one's *being* and all *doings.* Thus, **Total Personal Excellence** or **TOPEX**, is the very remarkable or extraordinary *Total Quality* of a *Person.* Such a person is thereby *exceptionally* good in his *Inner Being or Personality,* and thus also in his *Lifestyle* as well as his *Vocational*

Activity! Towards this realisation, every one of us has the *sacred indispensable duty* to fully develop all potentialities within himself to the fullest extent possible and to thereby consistently sustain them as valuable executive powers via a very effective process of **Continuous Personal Development, CPD**. Very strictly as ordained by the Almighty **LORD**, who has blessed every human spirit with the gifts of all natural talents they will require for their entire life in this Creation.

These talents, then, must be very diligently applied towards the right performance of one's *Vocation*, involving the Roles, Responsibilities and Duties by which one can surely *actualise* and *perfect* his own *Unique Meaning*, including both *essential* and *functional parts* while simultaneously ensuring the fulfilment of one's *prime essential purpose* of conscious existence here. Now, having stated the fact that **Total Personal Excellence, TOPEX**, naturally falls into three significant aspects, it is very important here to give some basic clarifications about each one in order to facilitate our clear and correct grasping of it. Let us, therefore, begin with the **Excellence of Personality**. We now know that *Excellence* is the quality of being *extraordinarily good* at something, up to the very best standards.

Therefore, *Excellence of Personality* can be defined as the state of being *exceptionally* good regarding the personal qualities or characteristics that define one's *Being*. Again, the personal qualities or characteristics in question here are those that derive directly from the *pure potentialities*, the natural *gifts* of the Almighty **CREATOR,** which were referred to earlier on. Correspondingly, the actual specified standards by which these are naturally assessed, verified, and judged are the absolutely pure and perfect **CUE LAWS** of the **ALMIGHTY** in this great **CREATION**. They are the most accurate *natural expressions* and *automatic executives* of the Holy Creative Will of the Great **LORD**, who is the *Sole* **Author** of and the *Supreme* **JUDGE** over all that be. And what exactly are those natural talents, the pure gifts of the Almighty **LORD** which we must promptly awaken, diligently nurture and perfect to full executive powers, required for attaining the highly valued **TOPEX?**

First of all, quite naturally, is man's *ego* or *being! That* is man's real self, the *living spiritual power* spark at the *core* of a person, which was brought into existence by the Holy Creative Will of the Almighty **LORD** through the Command **"Let There Be Light!".**

This *spiritual spark or ego*, also known as *spirit seed-grain*, which begins its living in paradise as an unconscious unit of life force, bears within itself the capacity to develop gradually first into a *human spirit* that is conscious of its own self, and then proceed to become a *real human being* who may thereby finally attain the *most blessed* status of a true ***'Child of GOD'*** by the very special grace of the **ALMIGHTY**. That gift of conscious existence in this great Creation of the **LORD** is the very first valuable gift He gave to His human spiritual creatures, and it is thus our most precious attribute!

Now, every human spirit has within it a ***Heart*** (i.e., a *living spiritual power centre*), through which it receives the *life-sustaining power currents* from the Almighty **SOURCE** of All Life and Being. These living currents always animate and maintain the *human spiritual heart*, plus all systems and processes of life within the human soul, together with those in the physical body, which is the outer physical covering and tool of the soul down here. It is naturally this very power centre, the ***Heart***, that keeps the human spirit alive and active, with the living power streaming through it from the **SOURCE** of all life, quite similar to how an *energised* dry cell *automobile battery* always activates all electrical and electronic systems and gadgets in an automobile here on Earth. Or else, on a grander scale, similar to how the *star* of our solar system, the mighty *Sun*, energises, activates and supports all bodies and all activities in this solar system, exactly as ordained by the great **CREATOR**.

This highly significant power centre within the human being also serves or powers all internal systems like the **Intuitive faculty**, sometimes simply called the **Intuition**. This one bears three *spiritual* abilities within it. Thus, the inner spiritual *Visual, Hearing* and *Sensing* abilities. It is by the combined activity of those three intuitive abilities that we can attain clear and correct *comprehension* of both inner and outer experiences at an exceedingly high speed. They also enable the experiencing of dreams and inspirations and the reception of high knowledge, instructions or guidance from the higher realms. Side by side and very closely linked to the *Intuitive faculty* is another very powerful gift of our **LORD.** The ***Conscience***! This is man's great spiritual faculty of *morality*, the natural *seat of ethics,* which enables one to clearly distinguish between what is *right* and what is *wrong* in our lives and activities, provided one always humbly allows himself to remain open to guidance from above! Precisely from the All-embracing Wisdom or Omniscience of the **ALMIGHTY**!

Now, working very closely with **Intuition**, this highly significant faculty really helps us to assess things very well by carefully weighing their pros and cons before making final decisions. It has been given to all of us by our Great **MAKER** to enable and support the correct use of our **Free Will Power**, a very great, highly essential ability by which we can make *conscious* and *independent* decisions and actions. To the outcomes of which we are then *most inescapably* bound and held *totally accountable* by the absolutely pure, perfect and incorruptible Justice of the **MOST HIGH**. In addition, there is the wonderful intelligent instrument, the human **Mind**, which is the faculty of human ***Consciousness*** that has its base naturally in and derives its motive force from the human spiritual **Heart**. Its own network of links or channels extends from there to cover all parts of the human soul and its physical body, with all corresponding systems.

These include the physical nervous system, the cardiovascular and blood circulatory systems, etc. With these powerful gifts also comes the spiritual **Memory**, a very powerful and tenacious eternal storage bank of all *genuine*, real-life experiences of the spirit in which the back brain of man, the *cerebellum*, plays a very vital role as a tool here on Earth. Thus, we must work very diligently to nurture and keep the latter alive and in very good health always! Another wonderful gift we have is the power of **Reflection**, which is the *collaborative* capacity that links our frontal *intellectual* brain to our Intuitive Faculty via our rear *intuitional brain* for processing of information in such a way that results in deeper insights about things. The frontal brain, cerebrum itself is the human thinking tool, a physical *thought-generating* tool of the spirit, linked to all of our bodily systems, organs, tissues and cells, as a result of which we are able to directly make sense of all processes going on within and outside of the physical body.

It is also the tool through which we express ourselves down here on Earth as human spirits, either by action or movement of our body or by speech via the very great and significant gift of **Language**; the ability to speak and express ourselves through vocalisation. And we must not forget the wonderful gifts of being able to manufacture, walk and run, see and hear, smell, and materially taste the blessings of our Great **MAKER** down here! So very many indeed are the special gifts of the Almighty **LORD,** which we tend to take *very much* and *too often* for granted instead of constantly and consistently sending our jubilant thanks upwards to Him in reverential Love. And do you know the greatest, highest and indeed the most highly significant gift that He has most graciously bestowed on all of us? A most essential gift, without which a human spirit is bound to become lost forever? It is indeed the *spiritual **Micro-Spark***, out of the living radiations of His **Truth**!

This particular gift naturally enables every one of us who *genuinely* and *seriously* longs for it to really establish and maintain a living reverential link with our great **MAKER**, the **Everlasting TRUTH** Himself! This gift helps to ensure that one will always be able to remain *inwardly connected* to and stride gradually upward toward Him. However, It is the constant and serious *longing* for the Almighty **LORD**, the **TRUTH**, and His heavenly Kingdom that actually enables each genuine seeker to attain this upward movement. For if one earnestly works for ***Self-consciousness*** while developing down here and makes the serious efforts to develop and sustain a very strong humble connection of pure *reverential love* for the **ALMIGHTY**, it really helps a great deal by ensuring one's joyful ascent to the luminous Paradise, our origin!

That is, of course, based upon one's attainment of full spiritual maturity and through the special grace of the great Love of the **MOST HIGH**. It is thus of utmost necessity that we must strive very seriously to develop all those natural talents bestowed upon us by the **ALMIGHTY**, up to full executive powers, which we can then diligently apply towards the attainment of the sought-after **TOPEX**, *Total Personal Excellence.*

With that said, let us now move on to examine the second aspect of **TOPEX**, which is called the **Excellence of Lifestyle**. The latter quite naturally arises directly from the first one (i.e., the *Excellence of Personality*) in precisely an *inside-out* fashion. This is when every visible or perceptible behaviour of its bearer naturally flows forth directly from the *Excellence* of his inner attitude, a personal quality that characterises his inner *Being.* Naturally, this may become obvious in the person's manner of speaking and the personal style of using the language, both verbally and bodily. It also manifests in his liaison and his interpersonal relationships with others. Indeed, there are so many other measures of this quality as reflected, for instance, in one's habitat or home, in the style of decoration with regard to the choice of objects, materials, shapes, sizes, and colours. And naturally also, in one's stance or style of standing, way of looking and manner of walking! Finally, again, there is the personal choice and style of dressing, etc.

Now, regarding this level of **TOPEX**, what is most essential is the very special attention that one pays to the **CUE LAW of Natural BEAUTY** by meticulously adjusting oneself to its principles of *Purity* and *Orderliness, Balanced Coordination, Harmony,* and *Noble Gracefulness.* This is very important because via one's own very careful self-adjustment to all these principles, one is thereby naturally honouring and glorifying the **ALMIGHTY**, whose wonderful CREATION always manifests His Glory in the *most exquisite* and very *beautiful* ways for us to learn from and adjust to! It is also via these principles of **Natural BEAUTY** that all personal abilities and qualities can be consciously brought forward to diligently influence the development of the next level of Excellence, **Vocational Excellence**.

Vocational Excellence! Through the already acquired **Excellence of Personality** and **Excellence of Lifestyle**, the person concerned can very confidently leverage and direct all his abilities towards the development and correct application of those *Vocational Competencies* required for performing his personally recognised, clearly defined

Roles, Responsibilities, and Duties, up to the very best *Standards of Excellence* in his chosen field of activity. And what are those Vocational *Competencies*? They are precisely the right *Vocational* Attitude and Knowledge, *accurate know-how*, plus sharp Vocational Skills, and *masterly can-do*, which at the same time will enable him, the *excellent role holder,* to precisely actualise the *unique meaning* of his being while also attaining those *High Life Goals* which most accurately constitute the true essence of his own *prime essential purpose* of conscious life down here in exact accordance with the All-wise, Holy Will of the Almighty **CREATOR**.

NOW, when the serious success-seeker has finally attained all three aspects of this great personal quality, **TOPEX**, there is *no chance again* of resting on that glory at all! The level of attainment *must* be well balanced and sustained through the process of *Continuous Personal Development* and *Improvement* in order to really ensure the lasting values. What we must bear in mind here, though, is that these come about for us only if we first and foremost strive earnestly to correctly develop those pure potentialities, the natural gifts of the **LORD**, in strict accordance with His Holy WILL for the good deeds for which they have been given to us. And that also demands very strict *self-adjustment* to His pure and perfect **CUE LAWS** that most accurately express and automatically execute this Holy Will in the whole of this great CREATION.

There are no *quick fixes* or *cutting corners* for any of us in these matters. For the **CUE LAWS** of the **MOST HIGH,** our **MAKER**, are absolutely very *stern*, *severe*, and exacting, and therefore utterly unbendable! Thus, before them, we can either humbly bend (i.e., adjust ourselves to them) or else painfully break! The choice is strictly ours alone! In addition, we *must* also very humbly obey His **Ten Commandments**, which form the *authentic explanation* and *practical interpretation* of His Holy Will. And for the simple fact that our own conception of *Excellence* is not the same, in any way or form, as His own, we must always seek His guidance in this regard as well.

The biblical reference: **"Your ways are not my ways, and neither are your thoughts the same as my thoughts!"** is very aptly applicable here. Therefore, if we earthmen really wish to attain the exceptional quality, **TOPEX**, which is the real essence of true lasting **SUCCESS** with lasting values in this life, we really must supplicate humbly to the Great **LORD** for His divine help. Every serious *success-seeker* must first and foremost ask that he may *be allowed* to become a *LifeLong Apprentice* of **His Holy Will** and must, as such, be prepared to *very humbly* listen and obey His divine instructions and guidance given to us in His **Living WORD**, via His *pure* and *perfect* **CUE LAWS**, with joyful and grateful enthusiasm! This, indeed, is how we can receive the strength and the support that we need to develop the very extraordinary quality of **TOPEX**, consciously and correctly. It then really shines through in the *winner*, powerfully and gloriously, in honour of the **MOST HIGH**. Let us now move on to examine those *Eternal Values* of **True Lasting SUCCESS**, which are presented next.

PART 7: The Eternal VALUES! – Fruits of True Lasting *SUCCESS* in this Life!

Dear fellow *success-seeker,* it is now very important to highlight those *Lasting Values, the Eternal Benefits* of true **SUCCESS**, which the earnest *seeker* acquires in the process of his very serious, consistent striving along the **GREAT SUCCESS HIGHWAY**. This is necessary for enabling the *seeker* to awaken the very crucial *self-motivation* within him. *This* really helps one to keep on *working consistently* towards his *Goals*. If we very firmly keep our desired outcomes in mind right from the start, we are enabled to retain a sharp and positive focus which most certainly ensures fulfilment. In reality, all of those *seven principles*, the *Essential Building Blocks* of true **SUCCESS**, which we examined earlier in part five of this book, are indeed parts of the *Lasting Values* attained by the winning *success-seeker.*

Remember those *Building Blocks*? We have **S**elf-Consciousness and **U**sefulness plus **C**ommitment**, C**ompetence, **E**nthusiasm and **S**elf-Control, and, finally, **S**teadfastness. Precisely as the *acronym* of these seven great principles very vividly spell out the highly significant concept, **SUCCESS**, so also do these principles themselves always unite, as developed *executive powers*, to forcefully impel their conscious and serious bearer from *within*, to resolutely pursue his *High Life Goals* towards total glorious fulfilment. The fact is, once these values have been developed as personal qualities or powers, they then remain as the intrinsic properties of their achiever permanently, for the rest of his life, *provided* he continually sharpens and *diligently* uses them exclusively for what is good and *just*. In fact, the latter condition, through its continuity, directly facilitates the growth of the valuable power of **Diligence**.

More importantly, the practice of continuously sharpening and diligently using the stated personal powers quite naturally enables the *Success-seeker* to retain and advance his own standing on the **GREAT SUCCESS HIGHWAY**! He will never fall off his own track but remains firmly anchored and steady therein. Very worthy of careful note is also the fact that it is while seriously working to develop the *value* of **Self-consciousness** that one is naturally enabled or helped to grasp the *true* **Recognition** of the All-wise Creative Will of the Almighty **CREATOR**, through which one has been able to come into conscious existence. It is through this very **Recognition** that one can then attain *true* **Recognition** of the Great **CREATOR Himself**, whereby one can proceed in earnest to develop a *strong* and *unshakable* **Conviction** of His *sublime* **BEING** through further real-life learning experiences.

Which then very powerfully moves the seeker within himself to seek the way to establish a *Proper Connection in a Bond of pure reverential Love* for the great **LORD**! This may be accompanied by a very strong urge, passionate wish, to become His **true Child**. The *greatest* living *value* of all, which can *absolutely only* be granted to the seeking one by the Almighty **LORD** alone, out of His great Love! It is very certain, though, that if a human being can grow progressively stronger in this volition and really strive to wholeheartedly *devote* himself to a definite *useful purpose* that truly lies in the Holy Will of the **MOST HIGH** down here, he will by the special grace of the **LORD** attain that status, a *true child* of the Almighty **LORD**, eventually.

The lasting benefits that naturally arise from this *Proper Connection* with the Almighty **LORD** include, in addition to those stated earlier on, the spiritual values of ***Inner light*** or ***Illumination***, with an awakened and clarified ***Intuitive Faculty*** plus an active **Conscience**. There comes also the happy liberation of the ***Will Power*** of man, which then grows ever stronger and more effective as it is fully and humbly aligned with the All-wise Holy Will of the Almighty **CREATOR**. Man's ***Spiritual Memory*** also gradually comes alive for the very necessary clearer and more vivid recollections of real-life events. And gradually, with all of these enabling Values, develop ***Self-Ennoblement*** and ***Spiritual Maturity***. The happy experience of ***Radiant Health, Unquenchable Strength*** and ***Joyful Vitality*** will naturally also be thereby enhanced, together with progressive ***Ascent***, which finally culminates in the glorious attainment of the very wonderful crown of all spiritual gains, the ***Blissful Eternal Life*** in the pure, luminous spiritual Kingdom... **Paradise**! As a very special and gracious gift of the great **LOVE** of our **ALMIGHTY LORD**.

The latter is the natural blissful consequence for every human being who very earnestly strives to acquire true ***Recognition*** of the Almighty **CREATOR** and to thereby build a very humble, strong and *intimate* **Relationship** with **HIM**, which is strictly based upon *pure* and *selfless* ***Reverential Love*** for **HIM**! This is all facilitated and firmly assured by genuine *self-adjustment* to His **Living Word** and therein also His All-Wise **Holy Will**. Thus, every serious *Success-seeker* who very *carefully* and *conscientiously* follows the *Wise Guidance* that is most graciously given to him in the **Living Word** of the **LORD** will surely find and be able to correctly follow his *own Purest Surest Path* upon the **GREAT SUCCESS HIGHWAY**, the Principled WAY of the **Almighty RULER** of All Realms, our **GOD**! May we all, each one by himself, be able to achieve this ardently longed-for **True Lasting SUCCESS** in this life by the *Very Special **Loving Grace** of the **MOST HIGH***!

AMEN!

BEFORE YOU GO – *A Serious Reminder!*

Fellow *Success-seeker!* As we now finally come to the end of this great *Exploration, I solemnly* wish to share with you the *serious essence* of the great *Motivating Principle* at the very heart of this work (i.e., **OUR MOTTO**). It is captioned below simply as:

"ALMIGHTY KING… FIRST AND FOREMOST… IN ALL ETERNITY!"

It derives from the very *highly significant* and *irrefutable* **FACT** that:

WITHOUT the *Divine Help* or *Support* of the Almighty **LORD**, our **GOD**, there is *neither any way* nor possibility whatever, absolutely, for any one of us here on this Earth, in the whole world, and the entire great Creation to achieve *True **SUCCESS*** with *Lasting Benefits!*

For there is Absolutely ONLY **One GOD**, ONLY **One Omnipotent-Omniscient LORD**, WHO by His **Supreme LAW** most *authoritatively* and *rightfully* Commands:

"I… AM THE LORD!… THY GOD!… THOU *MUST NOT HAVE*… ANY OTHER *GODS* BUT ME!"

And this, *most certainly, Absolutely Alone,* is the **Surest Mainspring** and the **Mainstay** of all *successful* manifestations, all processes, activities, movements and devel-opment towards fulfilments and perfection of all aspects of Life in the entire great **CREATION**, unto all eternity!

So, *first* and *foremost*, anyone who seriously desires *True Lasting* **SUCCESS** in this life *must* strive very seriously to completely and, very *humbly,* submit himself to this *highly significant* **Supreme LAW of the LORD**. With the *very crucial condition* that it must be taken strictly *together* with the other nine Commandments of the **LORD**. Because they collectively form an *absolutely inseparable,* integral whole that precisely explains and interprets the All-wise **Holy Will** of the Almighty **LORD**. Very clearly, in a practical, *unmistakable* language for all of us. It is indeed through *humble* and *most unreserved obedience* to this **Holy Will** that one can really honour the **ALMIGHTY**, exactly as He imperatively demands and justifiably expects of all His *human spiritual creatures,* by His stated **Supreme LAW**.

Thus, the *most urgent* and *highly crucial* need that we all have *right now* is to *earnestly* learn, *correctly* absorb and *humbly* obey these great **LAWS of the LORD** so that we can always diligently be, live and work accordingly. For therein only, *absolutely only,* lies the **Surest Pathway** of **True Lasting SUCCESS**, the **GREAT SUCCESS HIGHWAY** that we so ardently seek down here.

May the **ALMIGHTY KING**, our **LORD**, in His great **Love**, grant all of us, His *human spiritual creatures and… children,* the Strength we each require to attain it most gloriously. In His Honour and Glory, **AMEN**!

AND JUST A MINUTE! **A** *SACRED ASSERTION* COMES TO MIND:

'GOD IS GOD!'... THE ONLY POWER! AND THE LORD OF ALL THE WORLDS! ALL REALMS OF EXISTENCE!

IN ALL INTERNITY!... HE ABSOLUTELY ALL-EXCLUSIVELY ALONE!

'GOD IS GOD!'... ABSOLUTELY WORTHY OF PURE REVERENTIAL AND SELFLESS LOVE AND HUMBLE WORSHIP IS HE... FOREVER... AND EVER... AND EVER!

INSPIRATIONAL RESOURCES

1. **'In The Light Of Truth – The Grail Message' By Abd-Ru-Shin**
2. **'The Ten Commandments Of God And The Lord's Prayer' By Abd-Ru-Shin**
3. **The Life Of Jesus On Earth – From Past Millennia**
4. **Jesus Of Nazareth – Past Eras Awaken Vol Ii**
5. **The Life Of Jesus, The Son Of God – Past Eras Awaken Vol Iii**
6. **The New Testament – Holy Bible (Nkjv)**

Ola Usman
Alphinst Global
Nyk & Uk
18/10/2022

The author

Sikiru Usman, originally from Nigeria and now residing in Southeast London, retired as a Regional Training Coordinator at SENSE (The National Deafblind and Rubella Association). Married with a child, his diverse interests in nature, people, places, cultures, life enrichment, and personal development converge in his debut book, "The Great Success Highway."

This literary venture marks Sikiru's transition into authorship. He describes his book as a reliable guide for those seriously seeking lasting success. Emphasising personal responsibility, Sikiru invites readers onto a metaphorical highway, urging them to actively shape their journey towards true success. His work not only encapsulates a life rich in experiences but also serves as a beacon for individuals prepared to invest in their growth and development. His book is not just a guide; it's a call to action for those ready to embark on a fulfilling and lasting journey.